You Can Be Transformed!

A study of Luke: God's Gospel
of new life

Larry Richards

While this book is designed for reading enjoyment and personal profit, it also is intended as a resource for group study. A leader's guide is available at 75c from your local bookstore or from the publisher.

D0963487

Published by
VICTOR BOOKS
a division of SP Publications, Inc.

Library of Congress Catalog Card Number: 73-78691
ISBN: 0-88207-236-6
You Can Be Transformed!
© 1973, SP Publications, Inc. World rights reserved
Printed in the United States of America

CONTENTS

PART I

NEW LIFE FOR ALL

1
The
Desperate
Need

Had there been newspapers in the Roman Empire
almost 2,000 years ago, some of the headlines that
month might have been:

KING ARTAXUS NEAR DEATH
GRAIN SHIPS DOCK, ROME RIOTS
    AVERTED
NINE PIRATE SHIPS SUNK BY SIXTH
    FLEET
ATHENS STUDENTS CLASH WITH POLICE
OLYMPIC WRESTLER STILL IN COMA
REPORT ANGELS SIGHTED IN JUDEA

Such headlines look very much like the headlines
in our newspapers today. For the world of the
New Testament was a world much like ours.

There were wars.

There was sickness.

There was poverty and discrimination.

There was injustice.

There were people who struggled to keep on
living, living by habit long after they had lost any
sense of purpose, meaning, or goal.

It was a world like ours, with people like ours.

7

But God had made preparation. God was about to burst into this world of men. Jesus was about to be born, and after His birth this world, with all its wars and poverty and injustice, would never be the same.

The World That Was

God had never desired the kind of world men have made. The Bible tells us that God worked carefully with men, and "He looked for judgment, but behold! oppression; for righteousness, but behold a cry" (Isa. 5:7). Even the people of Israel, who had been given God's laws and the prophets to guide them, had twisted life out of shape. The people of Israel were brothers, but in the passion of selfishness they cheated one another, lied, and tried to use each other. Yet, the more life fell under the control of sin, the emptier life seemed, and the more frustrated people became (see Isa. 59).

So God judged the sin of His people. Now they lay crushed under the weight of the Roman empire; an empire that extended over the whole of the western world. Rome had brought peace . . . but with it heavy taxes, armies of mercenaries, Roman culture and values, the gladiatorial games, slavery . . . and even more misery.

There were still wars.

There was still poverty and discrimination.

There were still people who struggled to keep on living, living by habit long after they had lost all sense of purpose or meaning in life. Not all the power of the Roman Empire—nor all the progress of modern technology—have been able to satisfy the basic need of people to find life's meaning, and to break the bondage of sin that constantly expresses itself in individual life and society.

The birth of a Baby would now purport to do what no invention or authority of man could. Later that Baby, grown to manhood, would say "I am come that they might have life, and that they might have it more abundantly" (John 10:10).

In the person of Jesus Christ, God acted decisively to bring new life to individuals and to cultures. In the person of Jesus Christ, God presents an invitation to a new life! To every person who lives by habit, without direction or meaning or real hope —to you and to me—Jesus' birth offers a fresh newness, a life turned around and transformed by the power of God.

This is what the Gospel of Luke is all about: the transformed life. For Jesus is presented in Luke as the transformer, with a message of new life for all the world, and with a special message of new life for believers. As we trace through this exciting book together, we'll discover more and more what it means to *really live*. We'll learn the *how* of that abundant life Jesus promises: how that promise can be kept in our own daily experience.

And this we need to learn.

Desperately.

Responses to God's Involvement

The Old Testament foretold the coming of a day when God would step into this world of darkness to bring light and hope. A Child would be born, a Son given (Isa. 9:6), and that One would bear the name Immanuel, "with us is God!"

But the announcement that the time was at hand met with varied reactions.

Luke 1:5-25

Zacharias was a priest who lived in a little hillside town in Judea except when his shift was on duty at the Jerusalem temple. It was during one of these weeks of duty that he was chosen, by lot, to enter the Temple for the evening burning of incense. Entering, Zacharias was jolted to see an angel of the Lord standing beside the incense altar. Quieting Zacharias' fears, the angel told him that his prayers had been answered, and his childless wife would have a son, who was to be named John.

Zacharias' response to this announcement was one of hesitation and doubt. "How can I know this is true? I am an old man myself, and my wife is getting on in years . . ." *Zacharias' doubt was based on his understanding of nature.* He had failed to take God into account!

How often we hesitate to believe for the same reason. Answer *my* prayer? "Well, the way things normally work out. . . ." How wonderful that our God is not limited to the natural, or restricted to the usual! Our God is a God of the unusual, and the sooner we see Him as He is, the more quickly our lives will be transformed.

Certainly Zacharias should have seen the unusual in the angel's presence. Not only was John's birth announcement supernatural, everything said about the baby marked him off.

John's person. John was to be one of God's great men, a man filled with the Holy Spirit and set apart from birth (v. 15).

John's ministry. John was to turn many of his countrymen to God. The reference to "the spirit and power of Elijah" (v. 17) harkened back to a well-known Old Testament prophecy in Malachi 3. The angel's statement made it perfectly clear to anyone familiar with the Scriptures, as Zacharias must have been, that this baby was the forerunner of the promised Messiah. John's birth announcement was at the same time an announcement that God was at last ready to act—God was about to intervene in the world of men!

John's need. John's ministry involved preparation for the Messiah-Saviour's coming, and he would be used by God to "turn the hearts of . . . the disobedient to the wisdom of the just" (v. 17). How greatly such a ministry was needed is illustrated in his preaching (see Luke 3:1-20). There were many disobedient in John's day, as in ours. Many were uncaring, defrauded others, used violence or brutality to extort, lied for one another in court (see 3:12-14). John was to face this world of sin, and to prepare the hearts of men for the forgiveness and transformation that Jesus, who came after him, would bring.

Knowing all this from the angel's announcement, Zacharias still hesitated. He still doubted. And because of his hesitation, the angel Gabriel (vv. 19, 20), announced that he would be unable to speak until the day of John's birth.

After the months of silence, it came. John was born (1:57-66). Zacharias' tongue was loosed, and he praised God!

To some of us, faith comes only after hesitation. When it comes, how great is our praise.

Luke 1:26-55

The angel Gabriel had another announcement to make. Some months after he had spoken with Zacharias, Gabriel was sent to Nazareth, and there appeared to a young engaged woman named Mary.

Like Zacharias, Mary was startled and upset at the angel's appearance and his greeting. Reassuring her of God's love, the angel said that Mary would have a Son. This Son would be known as the "Son of the Most High"—"Most High" being one of the Old Testament names of the Lord. He would be of the Davidic line, and would be King over Israel, thus fulfilling all the Old Testament promises God had given to His people. In this one Person, then, deity and humanity would be perfectly blended and linked. In this one Person, all the promises of God to Israel and all the purposes of God for mankind would be fulfilled.

Like Zacharias, Mary was jolted into a question. "How can this be? I'm not married!" (v. 34). The angel's response echoed another Old Testament prophecy: "A virgin shall bear a child, and you will call His name Immanuel" (Isa. 7:14). There was to be no human father. The power of the Holy Spirit was to supernaturally invest an ovum with the germ of life, and the Child to be born would be God the Son (v. 35).

To this explanation Mary had only one response. "I belong to the Lord, body and soul. Let it happen as you say" (1:38, PH).

What a beautiful faith! Zacharias, godly and mature (see vv. 5, 6), had doubted the possibility of natural birth because of his age. This young girl, certainly still in her teens, never hesitated or questioned the *supernatural* birth, though she was single!

There is blessing for those of us who learn to believe in spite of doubt. There is even greater blessing for those of us who respond as Mary did, in perfect, childlike trust.

Mary's faith-response is even more striking when

we realize that, according to the Old Testament law, her pregnancy, while she was still single, might well be dealt with by stoning. And certainly her fiancé, who would know the Child could not be his, would hardly go through with the marriage. Yet all these things Mary was willing to trust to God to work out.

Instead of worry, joy filled Mary's heart. And her praise song, known as the Magnificat (vv. 46-55), is filled with praise for God and with a vivid awareness of His greatness and His love. What was Mary's vision of God?

He has done great things (v. 49).

Holy is His name (v. 49).

His mercy rests on those who fear Him (v. 50).

He has shown His strength (v. 51).

He lifts up the humble (v. 52).

He fills the hungry (v. 53).

He has revealed Himself (v. 55).

Mary knew God as a God of power and a God of concern. One who cares enough for the humble and the hungry to reach down and meet human need.

Perhaps this helps explain Mary's response of faith. She had a clear vision of God. She knew Him as a God who cares . . . and who cares enough to act. May we each come to know God so well!

The Birth of Hope
Luke 2:1-7

Mary's faith was not displaced. God spoke to her fiancé, Joseph (Matt. 1:19-21), and the marriage was completed, but not consummated.

As the time of Jesus' birth approached, Caesar Augustus declared an empirewide census. So all the people of Palestine went to the town of their birth to be registered. This brought Joseph and Mary, both of whom were of Davidic lineage, to Bethlehem. Though in the late stages of her pregnancy, Mary probably rode a donkey along the dusty roads and waited in weariness as Joseph tried to find accommodations when they reached their destination.

The inns were filled, but Joseph finally found a sheltered stable, possibly in a cave behind an inn. There, in the most common of circumstances, to the simple sounds of animals shifting their weight and munching their straw and contentedly swishing their tails, Jesus was born.

It was a strange, an unobtrusive birth for a King. No doctors crowded around, no gilt couch held the laboring mother, no fine linens covered the infant. In simplicity the Baby was born, broke the quiet with His cries, and His exhausted mother, her labors ceased, wrapped Him in a cloth and lay back to sleep, resting Him beside her where He could feel her warmth and be comforted by it.

We sometimes yearn for great and startling evidences of God's presence. "Oh," we think, "if only I could see miracles now, as in Bible days. If only something *great* would happen to me!" We long for the sensational.

How much we have to learn. For the greatest miracle of all, God's greatest work, was done in quietness and in the simplicity of a daily life common to millions upon millions of men. A look at the stable, and we may well wonder. Do the great things God wants to do in us and for us bear the same stamp? The stamp and seal of commonness . . . of God's mighty, yet unobtrusive, work in the lives of men?

Luke 2:8-20

But while the manger was silent, the hills resounded with shouts of joy. Far away, where it would not be observed by the crowds, a heavenly celebration was taking place. Choirs of angels shook the air with joyful shout and song, and as though unable to contain the good news, an angel appeared in a brilliant ball of light to shepherds in those fields, crying, "Good tidings . . . Unto you is born this day in the city of David a Saviour . . . Christ the Lord" (2:10, 11).

And why to shepherds?

Perhaps because they would understand. The Saviour, who was now born and lying in the quiet manger, was to be the Lamb of God. And as the Lamb, He was destined to die for the sins of the world. To die for these very shepherds as their Saviour. Perhaps shepherds, who cared for the young lambs, who sat through cold dark nights in the fields to guard and protect their flocks, might understand the shepherd's heart of God the Father, might glimpse what it meant for Him to give His one Lamb for all.

So as the hills throbbed and echoed with the remembered songs of joy, the shepherds left their sheep and hurried off to view God's Lamb.

They found Him. And they told Mary and Joseph of the angelic visitation. Leaving, they told everyone who would listen what the angels had said about this Child.

Luke 2:21-38

Once more before the years of silence, those years of the Saviour's growth to manhood in Nazareth, God gave the parents a special sign.

On the eighth day of Jesus' life on earth, the time for circumcision, Jesus was brought to the Temple to be presented to the Lord. Every first-born son was to be so presented, dedicated to the Lord and to His service. And then redeemed with a blood sacrifice: a young bull or a lamb for parents who could afford this offering, and for the poor, a pair of young birds. As Joseph and Mary moved to offer the sacrifice of the poor, they were met by Simeon, a man who had eagerly looked forward to the coming of the Saviour and had been shown by the Holy Spirit that this Child was to be He. Simeon took the baby Jesus in his arms, and praised God.

His praise was echoed by Anna, an 84-year-old widow who served the Lord in the Temple with prayer and praise, and who now told in all Jerusalem about Jesus, assuring them the Saviour had been born.

All this Mary stored up in her heart. She must have watched her Son as He grew; watched Him as He learned the trade of carpenter from His supposed father; watched as He moved in anonymity in an obscure town . . . watched, and wondered, and waited.

Now!
Luke 3:1-20

Then the days of obscurity came to an end. It began with John, who broke out of the desert like an old-time prophet, boldly announcing God's Word and challenging his hearers to a complete change of heart.

John's words were straightforward, and pierced to the hearts of his hearers. He called them a brood of snakes. He warned them not to keep on trusting in their ancestry; their own hearts must be right with God. When they cried out, asking what they should do, he told them plainly, and in the telling revealed the ways they hated and hurt one another.

The heart of John's message was simple: *there must be a change in your hearts.* God is about to act, judgment is coming. And you must have a new life!

There must be forgiveness first, for there has been sin. There must be baptism next, as 'a public sign of choice to turn from sin (3:3). And then there must be a whole new way of life—a new life that is in harmony with God and holiness, a new life that breaks completely with the ways of sin.

And John had one other message.

The Saviour-Messiah is coming. The One who will make all this possible for you is approaching. He will be here soon. You must be ready! (3:16)

Luke 3:21

And then Jesus came. He stood in the waters, and in baptism identified Himself with the people and with the stand for righteousness that this act symbolized. Then God's voice came from heaven: "This is My Son, My beloved, in whom I am well pleased."

And, being about 30 years old, Jesus began the work that was to bring the possibility of a truly new life to you and to me.

EXPLORE

To further explore this portion of Scripture and its meaning to you . . .

1. Look at headlines in today's papers. How do

they reflect the same needs and problems revealed in Luke 3:1-20?

2. How do you perceive God right now? Jot down
your images and ideas about Him.

3. Now study Mary's Magnificat (Luke 1:46-55).
Compare her view of God with what you have
jotted down. How are the two alike? Different?

4. This Book of Luke is about "new life." Write
down at least five things that you feel would
characterize a "new life" for you.

5. Before you go on in this book, ask God to use
His Word to help you discover the new life
Jesus has for you, and the abundant life He
wants to give you.

2

Trapped!

I first began to feel trapped when I was in high school. It all started well; I was running up a flight of stairs as a freshman and bumped into our football coach. When he got up, he said, "I can't wait till you come out for football!" I went out for football, but I was clumsy. I fought it out for a tackle position with a friend, Kayle Craig, and lost. He was a good guy, and I was glad for him. But it was embarrassing when he'd get his 5′2″ body underneath my 6′1″ frame and I'd flop like a beached whale.

So I went out for baseball, and discovered that every time I hit a pitch it popped softly 20 feet to the right of second base. Soon, in our practice games, seven guys on the other team would be standing there, waiting for the put out, which may have been the biggest overshift in baseball history. Fortunately, I got plantar warts on my right heel and was able to withdraw gracefully.

I had similar successes in social life. For one thing, I have very peculiar hair. It grows out a dozen different directions, and without Command or some greasy kid stuff, it earned me my nickname: Bushman. I still had my personality, of course, but that didn't help much. I was shy; so shy I couldn't look a girl from my class in the eye. If I were downtown and saw one coming, I'd cross the street, or look down, or find something interesting in a store window, just so I wouldn't have to greet her.

Things didn't change much in college. I did learn to play Ping-Pong. And once I took a girl on a long walk on a winter night in Yellow Springs, Ohio. We walked to the city dump, where we threw snowballs at the jumble of cans to hear the rats jump and scurry.

After two years I joined the Navy. A lot of things happened there. After two more years I became a Christian and joined a little Bible-preaching church. I felt a lot better. Before, I'd gone to movies on 42nd Street in Manhattan—two or three triple features a day—and been very lonely. Now I had Christian friends, decided to study for the ministry, became president of our youth group, and just before discharge met a special girl on a Saturday night, proposed the next Wednesday, and a few months later we got married.

It was a new beginning. But while living in our little house trailer in Saline, Mich., I discovered it wasn't going to be as I'd imagined. My boyhood home had been quiet; we didn't get excited. But my new wife felt things intensely, and expressed her feelings. When she did, I ran and hid, unable to help her or respond. I felt afraid.

Perhaps you've felt that way. Boxed in? Trapped? Struggling for freedom from your faults and weaknesses and for freedom to live successfully with loved ones and associates? If so, you feel the same need that I've felt; the need to break out of the traps, to find freedom, and to begin to really live.

So it's got to be exciting to discover that Jesus promises us new life: eternal life, *now*. And that even before Jesus began to talk to the men of His day about the new life He was offering, He gave them a demonstration of the power and the freedom He had—and that He came to bring to us all.

His Ancestry
Luke 3:23b-38

Ancestry was very important to the Jewish people. They traced their lineage back to Abraham. Their whole identity as a people rested on the fact that God had given promises to Abraham (Gen. 12, 15, 17) which they, as his descendants, had inherited.

While Jesus' sudden appearance in Judah was not supported at the time by genealogical evidence, both Luke and Matthew felt it was important to show that, on the human side of His nature, our Lord was both in the Abrahamic line of promise and in the Davidic royal line, and thus qualified to take the throne God had promised the Messiah.

Let's note just two things about the genealogy before moving on. First, as is common to biblical genealogies, this one skips. It does not necessarily record each generation; a "son of" someone, in Hebrew usage, might be a grandson or a great-grandson. Only the notable in the family need be mentioned. Thus we can't estimate times or dates by using Bible genealogies.

The second thing is that this genealogy differs in significant ways from the genealogy in Matthew. Why? Most Bible scholars believe that Luke gives the genealogy of Mary (who was also of the royal

Davidic line), while Matthew traces the line of Joseph. Thus, by both His mother and His supposed father, Jesus' right to the throne of Israel is established.

Luke 4:1-13

Even more important at this point in Jesus' life and ministry was the establishment of His claim to be the Transformer, One who could bring a new kind of life to people. So before Jesus would offer others new life, *He would prove in a personal demonstration that new life was possible.*

Jesus would show His own freedom from that inadequacy and sin which trap you and me, and in proving that freedom is possible, would give us fresh hope.

The First Temptation
Luke 4:1-4

Jesus was led by God after His baptism (Luke 3: 21, 22) into the desertlike country where no one lived. He was there for 40 days to be tested.

Jesus had to prove that new life was reality in Him.

Those were hard days for the 30-year-old Nazarene. He ate nothing during the 40 days, and the Bible says He was hungry afterward (4:2). Physically, He was drained of the natural resources inherent in our bodies. It was then that the devil came to Him with the first temptation. There are several things to note about this first temptation.

"If You are the Son of God . . ." Satan initiated his attack, not by asking a question, but by making a statement.

There are a number of uses of *if* in every language, but the Greek language usually makes clear the kind of *if* that's meant. One *if* means doubt: "Well, if you think so, but I can't see it myself."

Another *if* means *since*. Suppose an employer comes home every day from work and complains about a particular secretary. She's inefficient. She comes to work late. She misfiles things. Finally his wife gets so upset she blurts out, "Well, *if* you're the boss, why don't you fire her?"

This *if* says *since*. Because you are the boss, act like the boss!

This is the kind of *if* that Satan uses here. "Since You are the Son of God, act like God and command these stones be made bread!"

Man. Jesus' response is a thrilling one for you and me. He quotes a Scripture that says, "Man shall not live by bread alone." In selecting this particular verse, Jesus identifies Himself with us, and clearly defines the battlefield. *Jesus will not face the testings of Satan in His deity; Jesus will meet each test as a man.*

In this we find hope. If Jesus had responded to temptation in His divine nature, there would have been no help here for you or me. His victory would have proved nothing but that God is greater than Satan, that God is free. But Jesus came into this world to live as a man. To be hungry and tired and misunderstood and hurt, as we all have been. And Jesus met every temptation *as a man.* In His victory, He shows us the possibility of victory too.

What Jesus did as a man, using the resources available to every believer, *we* can do. The principles on which Jesus' victory was based are principles by which you and I can live. And by which we can be freed from the things that trap us.

Scripture. The next thing to note is that to find victory Jesus went to Scripture, and used God's Word in a particular way.

As a young Christian, I was told that the Bible would give me victory over sin. Yet I was gripped by a particular temptation. I'd quote a verse that I thought was appropriate when I felt the surge of my temptation. But as soon as I stopped quoting, I'd always immediately give in.

I was using the Bible as something like Hindu prayer beads, saying words over and over by rote as though there were something magical in the words themselves.

Jesus' use of Scripture was very different. He went back to the Old Testament, saying in effect, "Here is a principle to live by . . . and I will live by it." *He determined to act on what God's Word revealed to be God's will.*

So it always must be with the Bible. God's Word is given us to *live.* We are to be hearers, but not only hearers. We are to be doers also (James 1:22). In doing God's Word, Jesus found His freedom, and we will find ours.

The principle. This particular temptation of Satan was focused on the physical nature. Jesus, as a man who had fasted 40 days, was hungry. In response to the temptation, Jesus recalled, "Man shall not live by bread alone, but by every Word of God." Jesus had been led into the wilderness by the Spirit. He had been led to fast. Now He would not let His physical urges or needs dominate: He would choose instead to continue to do the will of God.

The physical is one avenue of temptation for all of us. Often those of us who are overweight let the demands of hunger rule us. Others are in the grip of sexual appetites. A young man and his wife felt led by God to go to a Texas seminary. They arrived and settled into a small seminary apartment in August, as the temperature hovered over 100° daily. In four days they decided God hadn't called them to *this* school; it was simply too hot.

Yet you and I are more than bodies. We're more than our sensations. Life for us is far more than the satisfaction of bodily urges and needs. For all of us who feel trapped in a pleasure-seeking culture, dominated by our desires, Jesus' victory offers us new hope. *The physical need not dominate our lives, either.*

With God's help, we can choose to live by His Word.

The Second Temptation
Luke 4:5-8

In the second temptation, Satan approached Jesus from a different direction. He showed Him all the kingdoms of the world in a moment of time, and offered them and their glory to the Messiah-King, if He would only bow down now to Satan.

Some have felt that this temptation involves worldliness—and have defined worldliness as a desire to possess things and as the pride of possession. Yet there is far more involved in the test than this.

A good thing. First of all we have to realize that authority over all the kingdoms of this world and possession of all their glory is Jesus' destiny. He is King of Kings (1 Tim. 6:15), and to Him one day every knee shall bow and every tongue confess that Jesus Christ is Lord to the glory of God the Father (Phil. 2:11).

Certainly what God has planned for Jesus can

not be, in itself, a bad thing—or worldly.

We have to believe, also, that it would be a good thing for us to have Jesus rule. Would there be wars and killings today if Jesus were in charge? Would there be sickness or cancer? Would there be crime, or discrimination, or injustice? Never! For the Bible says, "Of the increase of His government and peace there shall be no end, upon the throne of David and upon His kingdom, to order it, and to establish it with judgment and with justice from henceforth even for ever" (Isa. 9:7). The history of the world would have been very different if Jesus had surrendered to Satan's temptation—there would have been peace. There would have been good things.

But this was just the strength of the temptation. It was compelling, because what was offered *was* good!

Powerful temptations. It's not strange when we think about it. The most powerful temptations are those that involve good things. Not many of us would be tempted if someone said, "Hey, come on. Let's go out and commit a murder." Or, "Hey, let's go have a drunken orgy." Or, "Hey, let's go worship Satan." It is the good that tempts most of us.

When Marv was invited to move to Illinois from California, he was troubled by one thing. He had no winter clothes for his three young children and no money to buy any. Could he move and expose his children to this kind of danger?

When I graduated from seminary, I had hoped to go west. My wife has always suffered from allergies, and suffered terribly in Dallas. When an invitation came to move to Wheaton, Ill., to work with Scripture Press, we checked with an allergist in Chicago. His advice? "Don't come. The area would be bad for your wife."

Both Marv and we faced temptations involving good things. Isn't it good to consider the welfare of your children? Isn't it good to love your wife and to do what will keep her most healthy?

The good things put far more pressure of temptation on us all than do the bad!

God's will. How did Jesus respond to this temptation? He again returned to Scripture, and drew out a principle on which He was ready to stake His life. "Thou shalt worship the Lord thy God, and Him only shalt thou serve" (v. 8). He would not worship Satan; God only is to be worshiped. *And He would not serve the good; God's will alone is to determine!*

Choosing God's will cost Jesus Christ. Yes, God intended and still intends to give Him all kingdoms of this world and all their authority. But the pathway to the crown led Jesus by way of a cross. Suffering came before glory. Knowing this, Jesus turned His back on the good, and chose to live by God's will.

We know, of course, that the Cross brought a greater good. Jesus might have brought peace on earth as King; as dying Saviour, He brought peace with God and eternal life. All the suffering was worth it! God had our greater good in mind as He directed Jesus toward the scourgings and the thorny crown and the brutal pain of nails driven into yielding flesh.

It's always this way. God's will brings the greater good. Marv chose to bring his toddlers to Illinois, and though they had no money, warm clothing came as a gift. God took care of His own. I chose to bring my wife to Wheaton—and for several years there she was much improved. When her health began to go downhill again, we were led by God to first spend summers in Arizona, then to move here permanently.

We can never lose by choosing God's will. And we can never gain by choosing what seems good, if it is not His plan and purpose for us.

Jesus showed us the way to this victory too. Are you confronted by a *good thing* that attracts you? Then find your freedom to do the *right thing*, by determining that you, like Christ, will worship the Lord your God, *and Him only will you serve*. The choice to let God's will determine brings freedom.

The Third Temptation
Luke 4:9-12

The third temptation is particularly subtle and difficult to understand. Perched on the pinnacle of the Temple with Jesus, Satan challenged Him to leap off, reminding Him that, "If Thou be the Son of God," angels would appear to save Him from even dashing a foot against the stones below.

What was the nature of this temptation? Was it to demonstrate too soon a miracle that might gain attention and give Jesus a special hearing?

A different "if." The key to understanding this test is found in realizing that the *if* in Satan's challenge in verse 9 is not the *since* of verse 3, and in remembering that Jesus faced each temptation as a human being. As a human being, the 40 days of hunger, capped by the appearance of Satan to test Him, must have struck Jesus with wonder, and perhaps even with doubt!

Picture a similar situation. Suppose you feel led by God to go to the nearest airport to buy a ticket for Florida. You get off at Orlando, and the Lord seems to lead you to get into a taxi and head out of town. As you drive, you feel led to get out of the cab, and walk down a deserted lane. Finally, surrounded by scrub and sand and shallow waters, you sit down . . . expectantly. This has been the most unusual experience of your life! How often does God lead a person the way He has just led you? He must have something exciting in mind! And so you wait for it.

And you wait.

Night comes.

Finally comes morning. And you wait.

Another night. And another day. And you're still waiting. Hungry. Bitten by bugs. Alone. Nothing happening. *How long before you'll begin to wonder?* How long before you begin to think, "Now, did God really lead me out here, or was it my imagination?" How long before you yearn for some proof that God has been directing you and is still with you?

It was at just such a time as this that Satan addressed Jesus, "If (and here we have an *if* of hesitant doubt) You really are the Son of God, throw Yourself down."

"Why not settle it?" the passage implies. "You know that God won't let His Son come to harm. Prove to Yourself the relationship You claim, once and for all."

The Scripture. It's difficult to even suggest this interpretation of the final temptation. For one hesitates to believe that, even in His human nature, Jesus might have been subject to doubts. But look at the passage the Saviour now quotes. He returns again to the Old Testament, to Deuteronomy, and says, "You shall not put the Lord your God to the test" (Deut. 6:16, NASB).

To what is the passage in Deuteronomy referring? To a time when God's people had been led out of Egypt and given demonstration after demonstration of God's power and His care for them. Yet when they ran out of water, they cried, "Is the Lord among us, or not?" (Ex. 17:7). In so questioning God's presence and His care, they "put God to the test."

It was to just this kind of action Satan tried to tempt the Saviour: to make God prove Himself. And through Jesus, God's Word comes clear: "Thou shalt not put the Lord, your God, to the test" (see v. 12). *Relationship with God must always rest on faith, and on confidence in God's trustworthiness.*

How subject we are to this avenue of temptation! How quickly, when troubles come, we begin to doubt God, and question His love! How quickly, when a decision we've made brings strain, do we say, "Is God still with us? Did I make a mistake?" When under such pressures, how much we need to remember the principle that Jesus applied, and through which He found freedom to live victoriously: *in our relationship with God, faith is demanded.* We can trust God. We are not to test Him.

Peace . . . For a While
Luke 4:13

The temptations were now over for a little while. Throughout Jesus' life on earth, Satan would attack Him. But our Lord had demonstrated and would continue to demonstrate that, while He felt the pressures of the temptations as we do (see Heb. 4:15), still He was free from their power.

The power of a unique life was His. And it can be ours! For the power of His own unique life is exactly what Jesus offers to all who follow Him, and who choose to live His way.

EXPLORE

To further explore this portion of Scripture and its meaning to you, complete the following chart and use it to analyze temptations you may be feeling just now.

Avenue of Testing	My Problems in This Area	How Can I Apply Victory Principles?
The Physical physical instincts, desires, needs		
The "Good" letting something besides an appeal to God's will determine our choices		
Doubt failure to trust God when things are difficult		

3

The
Lifegiver

Germs?

For years the medical world laughed at the germ theory, the notion that infection and diseases are caused by tiny organisms no one can see. They questioned the need for special cleanliness and antiseptics in hospitals, and derided Pasteur and other early proponents of the germ theory.

It was so hard, later, to come to the man they had rejected and to admit: "You were right. We were wrong."

It's always hard to face a person who has been right when we've been wrong, and honestly to admit it—especially if what he has been right about is something important. Oh, I can admit to one of my children, "You were right. It was the 14th of July that the Bastille fell in the French Revolution." This doesn't hurt: it doesn't strike at my identity in any way. But how much harder to admit, "Son, you were right. I didn't have any real reason to say you couldn't go out. I was just feeling angry, and took it out on you. I'm sorry." This kind of admission is much harder: it hits at something important to me, my desire to be a loving and a fair dad, and to be viewed this way by my boys and girl.

It was this tough kind of admission—the admission of being *wrong* about something basic and important to their identity as Israelites—that Jesus now set out to call from the hearts of His people. As Jesus entered the first phase of His public ministry (Luke 4:14—9:17), He presented Himself as Lifegiver. To accept Him, people would have to admit that what they had known was not really life. Jesus would present a striking picture of life as it is to be lived in God. To accept *this,* people would have to admit that what they were now living was not God's way of life.

These admissions would be hard for them.

They're hard for us!

For in effect you and I, as we follow Jesus' ministry through the Scriptures, are faced with exactly the same choices that faced His contemporaries! As we look in these next two chapters at the real self of the Lifegiver and at the way of life He presents, you and I too will be forced to choose.

Rejection!
Luke 4:14-30

As Jesus began to teach and minister in the power of the Holy Spirit, there was an initial reaction of great enthusiasm (vv. 14, 15). People across the tiny country of Israel began to talk about Him with great admiration.

We don't know how long it was before He made a visit to Nazareth, His hometown, but certainly all there had heard of His successes. As a mark of courtesy, the ruler of the synagogue had even asked this young Man to read from the Scriptures. Unrolling the heavy scroll, Jesus found a place in Isaiah in which the ministry of the expected Messiah was described, a portion recognized by His hearers as Messianic.

"The Spirit of the Lord is upon Me . . .," Jesus read. "He hath sent Me . . . to preach the acceptable year of the Lord." And then He told them plainly: "This day is this Scripture fulfilled in your ears" (vv. 18-21). *This was the clearest possible claim that He, the carpenter who had worked among them, was in fact the long-promised Messiah, the Son of God!*

Hesitation. His claim seemed to stun them. They were drawn to Him and to His words (v. 22), but over and over they kept saying, "Isn't this Joseph's son? We've known Him as a child, a youth, a young man moving among us. Are we now to suddenly see Him as Israel's Deliverer?"

People today are faced with this same dilemma. Many have thought of Jesus as a teacher, as a good man, or as a tragic historical figure who was killed because He was too far ahead of His time. But when they meet Jesus in Scripture and hear His claims, they realize that He is asking them to see Him as the Living Son of God!

"Isn't this just a man, as we are?" There is no more critical question demanding an answer from us today!

Hard truth. Jesus understood their reaction. And He quickly confronted them with a picture of their attitude—and God's response to it. He told them in effect, "You'll want proof. Well, remember that in Israel's history, prophets have regularly been rejected in their own country, and that despised foreigners have had more faith and seen greater evidences of the mighty power of God" (see vv. 24-27).

There is no time for hesitation. Look, and choose, while you have the opportunity!

The choice. Confronted this way by things they did not want to hear—but which were impossible to refute because their very Scriptures recorded the events to which Jesus referred—all in the synagogue "were filled with wrath" (v. 28). And they tried to kill Him (v. 29).

In their reaction and in their choice, we see in cameo a portrait of Jesus' whole ministry. "He came unto His own," John tells us, "and His own received Him not" (John 1:11). The scene in Nazareth was reenacted over the next three years with the whole nation of Israel. In the end the furious anger roused expressed itself in implacable hatred, and led to Jesus' agony on the cross.

Thus the theme is set for this section of the Gospel of Luke: the theme of choice and rejection. Jesus will present Himself to His own people. They will see Him as He is. Yet, filled with hatred, they will strike out, desperate to destroy Him.

And we must be careful that our reaction to Jesus does not parallel theirs. When we see Jesus, when we come to recognize Him as the Son of God, we are forced to reject either ourselves or Him. We're forced to realize that apart from the Saviour we do not know life, and to admit our emptiness and need and such admission is likely to stick in our throats. Or we must reject Him and His claims. How terrible in such rejection to take a stand with the men of His day who hated Him, men who tried so desperately to quiet their own consciences by making Him go away!

Who Is This Man?
Luke 4:31—5:32

As Jesus moved from His home district into Galilee and Judea, a pattern began to develop in His ministry. He taught . . . but He also acted. And every action gave more and more dramatic proof of His power and Lordship.

Luke 4:31-41

Jesus began by demonstrating His authority over the outer things that bind men.

When a man under the control of a demon cried out in a synagogue where Jesus was teaching and identified Him publicly as God's Holy One (v. 34), Jesus spoke sharply to the demon and expelled it, freeing the man of the occult influence.

We've been used to discounting the power of Satan. Some Christians even question the existence of demons as living personalities. Scripture has no such question. In our own country today spiritualism and the occult are growing in popularity. The reality of demon influence and demon possession is being recognized, and experienced!

How wonderful it is to know that the Son of God has authority over the powers of darkness! And how amazed the people who watched Jesus were! "What's this!" they kept saying. "He commands the unclean spirits with authority and power . . . and they come out" (see v. 36).

Moving to the home of Simon, Jesus healed Simon's mother-in-law of a high fever. She recovered fully and began to serve Him and His companions. When men brought others to Him, He healed them of every kind of disease and expelled more evil spirits.

He needed no testimony from demons to the fact that He was the Son of God (v. 41). His every action gave stark miraculous witness that He could only be the Christ.

Luke 4:42-44

The crowds tried to keep Him with them the next day. But He moved on to other towns. All must see and hear Him. All must know the good news. The promised Kingdom was at hand. The King had come!

Luke 5:1-11

All had been amazed at Jesus' teaching and His power. Yet most still hesitated, waiting for more evidence or for some sign before they committed themselves to Him. But some did not hesitate. Some made the choice immediately . . . and with it the confession that choice must involve.

One day as Jesus was teaching near the shore of Lake Gennesaret (the Sea of Galilee), He was overwhelmed by the pressure of the crowds who thronged Him. He got in the boat of a fisherman, and from it continued to teach. When He was done He told the boat owner, Simon (who would later be called Peter), to push out into deep water and let down his nets.

By all odds this would be a futile action. The fishermen of Palestine worked at night, when the schools of fish worked in toward shore to feed on the swarms of minnows that sought their food and safety in the shallower waters. But Simon did as Jesus told him, and an enormous shoal of fish swarmed into their nets. Their nets began to break with the weight. When a second boat joined them, both were so filled that they nearly sank.

The final, simple evidence of Jesus' power was enough for Simon. He fell on his knees before Jesus. "Keep away from me, Lord, for I'm only a sinful man" (5:8, PH).

Recognition. Staggered by the haul of fish, Simon was jolted into recognition of Jesus as Lord. There were no questions left in the mind of this simple fisherman.

It may seem strange that the greater miracles of healing and expelling demons had not moved Simon earlier. Sometimes it is the simplest things that bring a person to realize that Jesus Christ is Lord. By whatever agency, how vital that we do realize, as Peter did, just who Jesus is.

Confession. Seeing Jesus also brought to Simon a vivid picture of himself. Beside Jesus, Peter stood revealed as "only a sinful man." Perhaps when you and I compare ourselves with other people, we might have some cause to boast. But when we compare ourselves to Jesus, we see our sin revealed in the light of His perfect purity. Knowing himself, Simon confessed his lack of life and goodness, and his need.

This is the confession that seems so hard to make—until we have made it. Until we discover in our own experience that once the admission of sin and need is wrung from our unwilling lips, we're made free, to find in Christ a life we've never known.

Invitation. And Jesus' response to Simon's confession? Invitation. "Don't fear. From now on you will catch men" (see v. 10).

From now on, life will be different!

Peter and his two companions left everything there on the beach—including the great catch of

fish—and followed Jesus. All that had been impor-
tant to them before was now willingly set aside.
In the fulfillment found in relationship with Jesus
Christ, all of life had truly become new.

Luke 5:12-32

Not all who saw Jesus' works and heard His teaching responded as Simon and his friends. So Jesus
moved on to show graphically that His authority
extended to the healing of the inner man as well
as the outer man.

Love. In Luke 5:12-16, we have a touching story
that focuses our attention on the inner needs of
men, and reveals Jesus' concern that these needs
be met.

A leper came to Jesus and fell down in front of
Him, saying, "Lord, if You want to, You can make
me clean" (see v. 12). He trusted Jesus' power, but
was uncertain of Jesus' love.

We're all so prone to using others. Some give
generously . . . to buy a reputation as generous.
Some may even show up for church visitation, to
be known by others as "faithful" and as "soul win-
ners." And so it was a fair question: was Jesus
using the people He healed to build a reputation
as a healer?

Jesus answered the implied doubt fully. He said,
"I want to." And then as He spoke the healing
word, Jesus reached out His hand, *and touched the
leper* (see v. 13).

Lepers in Jesus' day, as in ours, were untouchable.
They had to cry out in the streets, to warn others
away from them. They lived outside the cities, separated from their loved ones and families. They
were alone . . . and destined not to know the

loving caress or gentle pressure of another's hand.
And Jesus reached out and touched the leper.

If you've ever been lonely, ever felt rejected or
unloved, you know what that touch must have
meant. If you've ever been convinced that no one
could possibly care for you, then you understand
how that leper must have felt. Jesus' touch was not
needed to heal the leprosy, but it was necessary
to meet the man's deepest need which was for love.

Later, the leper would go and show his body to
the priests, and when pronounced clean of his
disease offer the prescribed offerings. What he
would not show them was his heart. His heart had
been healed too—it had known the touch of love.

If you've hesitated to trust Jesus, if you've been
convinced of His power but uncertain about His
concern, look again at the leper.

Jesus touched him.

Jesus wants to touch you.

Forgiveness. Luke moves on to describe Jesus'
working in the inner man in 5:17-26.

Many were gathered to hear Jesus teach, including religious leaders who were to be His implacable
enemies. When a paralyzed man was ingeniously
brought to Jesus over the dense crowd, Jesus recognized faith, and said to the man, "Your sins are
forgiven" (see v. 20).

The religious leaders, the scribes and Pharisees,
immediately grasped the implication of this statement. Jesus was claiming to be God! "Who can
forgive sins, but God alone?" (v. 21) Responding
to their unspoken thoughts, Jesus asked them
bluntly which was harder, to say, "Your sins are
forgiven," or to say, "Get up and walk" to a paralyzed man. Clearly the latter is more difficult. If
one says, "Get up and walk," all will know immedi-

ately whether the person who speaks has the power to heal. But who can know about one's authority to say, "Your sins are forgiven?" Forgiveness gives no unmistakable, visible evidence.

Jesus continued, "That ye may know that the Son of man hath power upon earth to forgive sins. (He said unto the sick of the palsy,) I say unto thee, Arise, and take up thy couch and go into thine house" (v. 24). Immediately the sick man got up, picked up his pallet, and went home, glorifying God all the way.

What lessons there are for us here! Jesus was touched by the physical need expressed in the paralysis, but His first concern was for the spiritual needs. For forgiveness of sins.

Sometimes we think that our greatest needs are for healing, or friendship, or finances. Jesus helps us penetrate to the heart of life's issue: our first need is for forgiveness and for a transformed heart.

Transformed? Jesus had asked the Pharisees, "Which is easier to demonstrate: power to heal, or authority to forgive?" It was clear that power to heal is easiest to show. But let's never forget that forgiveness also is expressed in a person's behavior!

Levi had been a tax gatherer (vv. 27-32). He was hated, because in those days men paid the government for the right to collect taxes, and were expected to collect far more than was due! Tax gatherers in Jesus' day were swindlers, quick to defraud, money-hungry, despised as collaborators with a foreign occupying force. Levi was one of these men, and he deserved his reputation.

But Jesus confronted Levi one day and standing eye to eye commanded, "Follow Me." And Levi followed!

Later Levi gave a party to introduce Jesus to

his friends, the outcasts of society like himself. The Pharisees and scribes muttered indignantly about Jesus' stopping to eat with such people. No doubt they were secretly delighted to have some apparent cause for criticizing Him.

Jesus' answer was sharp: Who is it that calls for a doctor? The one who is sick. And so He chose to be with those who saw themselves as sinners, recognizing their need. He could not reach the "righteous," who pretended they were well.

But what happens when Jesus touches the life of a man like Levi? What happens when a sinner follows Him?

Scripture gives us the answer. Turn back the pages of your New Testament and find its first book, Matthew. As you page through it, pause with me to wonder, for the man who wrote it, whom we know as Matthew the Apostle of our Lord, was once known as Levi.

If we had known him then, as Levi, you and I would probably have despised him too.

But how great a God we have! A God who cares about the despised. A God who can touch the hardest heart with His forgiveness, and transform the most warped personality—that the sinner might become a new man.

This is our destiny, too, yours and mine. If we come to Jesus, open our lives to confess our need and to receive His forgiveness, He will begin a change in us that will end in our transformation. In Him, life can become new.

He Stands as Lord
Luke 5:33—6:11

Jesus had demonstrated who He was. How did

those around react as He stood revealed as Lord?

Many hesitated. Jesus recognized the natural hesitation of men to try the new. In the illustration of the new wine (5:33-39), He noted that one who has been drinking an old wine will hesitate to turn to the new. He'll say, "The old is good." But the old after a time turns sour. When it is time for the new, even the skins (used in Jesus' day as bottles) must be fresh and new.

Jesus' coming was the bringing in of the new. Men now had to choose the new, or find the old turning sour on their tongues.

Others criticized. The leaders, particularly, tried to find fault. When Jesus' disciples plucked grain to eat on the Sabbath, the leaders felt that God's Law, as they interpreted it, was being violated. But Jesus responded: "I am Lord of the Sabbath" (see 6:5).

Some hated. On another Sabbath the religious leaders had planned a trap. A man with a withered hand was in the synagogue, and the Pharisees watched closely to see if Jesus would heal on the Sabbath. Jesus knew their antagonism and their thoughts (6:8). He called the cripple out in front of them all and, asking whether God's Law commanded doing good to others or harm, He healed him (6:9, 10). How could they meet His gaze (6:10)? They had no concern for the man they had tried to use against Jesus; he was merely a pawn to them. By His action, Jesus revealed to everyone the total hypocrisy and emptiness of all their pretentious claim to religious superiority. These were empty men, who loved only their own place and pride, and who were untouched by the hurts of those around them.

Jesus' actions revealed their hearts to others, and

to themselves. And they hated Him for it. "They were filled with insane fury, and kept discussing with each other what they could do to Jesus" (6:11, PH).

The Choice
Luke 6:12-19

The lines were being drawn. The crowds still hesitated. The leaders were becoming hardened in their hatred and rejection.

Jesus, after a night of prayer, selected to be His special disciples 12 of the men who had chosen to follow Him.

They had few qualifications. They had little education. No important family connections. Some had dark pasts. There were fishermen. A tax collector. Men of quick temper. But Jesus chose them to be with Him. These men had believed in Him, and been moved to confession and to trust. He was the King. He was the Messiah. He was the Son of God.

Jesus now marked out these men to be His disciples, and in following Him they would find the fullness of that transformation He promises to us all.

What different groups of men!

The crowds, who hesitated.

The leaders, whose pride led them to hatred.

The disciples, who in simple faith had stepped out on the pathway to transformed lives.

Which group are you in just now? Hesitating? Antagonistic? Or ready right now to take your place in confession as a sinner at the feet of Jesus, and ready to follow Him into the fulness of new life?

EXPLORE

To further explore this portion of Scripture and its meaning for you . . .

1. Think of a specific time when you had to admit you were wrong and say, "I'm sorry." How did you feel in that situation? Was it hard? Why? If not, what made it easier?

2. Jesus showed His authority in many ways. Skim Luke 4:31—5:32, and make a list of everything that you feel is evidence of who Jesus is.

3. Study carefully the "conversion" of Peter (5:1-11). What might have helped him make his confession? How does seeing Jesus' response (5:10) make it easier for *us* to come to Jesus as Peter did?

4. Put yourself in the place of the leper (Luke 5:12, 13). If you were to come to Jesus now, what would be your greatest *outer* need? What would be your greatest *inner* need? From this incident, how do you think Jesus would respond to you?

5. Right now, if you were to place yourself in one of the three groups distinguished at the end of this chapter, where would you be?
   —in the crowd . . . still hesitating, but listening?
   —with the leaders . . . antagonistic to Jesus and His claims?
   —with the disciples . . . forgiven, and ready to follow Jesus into an adventurous new life?

4

The
Ideal

Sometimes it's hard to form a picture of what living—really living—is like.

At a college days program this past year at Fort Wayne (Ind.) Bible College, I acted out a few of the ideas that people sometimes have. Listen to the dialogue in these skits, and see if any is familiar.

❖ ❖ ❖ ❖ ❖ ❖

Nurmi Catchitori, long hair, mustache, no bath.
Larry: "Uh, what are *you* doing here?"
Nurmi: "Man, I wanna begin to live. I just gotta, like, break outa my traps. What's it all about, hey?"
Larry: "You want to begin to live?"
Nurmi: "Yeah, I wanna, like, begin to really live."
Larry: OK. Here's how. First, cut your hair down to three inches. Then shave. Throw those clothes away. And start saying 'Yes, sir' to everyone older than you are. And smile when you say it."
Nurmi: "That's beginning to live?"
Larry: "Right on!"
Nurmi: "Yessir!"

❖ ❖ ❖ ❖ ❖ ❖

Joy, really sharp, smiling, looking like her name.

Joy: "I really want to begin to live. What do I do?"

Larry: "Well, do you ever smoke?"

Joy: "Some."

Larry: "Stop. Do you like to go to movies? To stay up late?"

Joy: "Yes."

Larry: "Stop, and get to bed by 9. Do you like housework?"

Joy: "No, I want to be a dean at a college."

Larry: "Grab a mop, woman. And clean."

Joy: "And that's beginning to live?"

Larry: "Yes. And by the way, remember, your dresses are supposed to be two inches below the ankles."

* * * * *

John, a mild looking, conservatively dressed guy, whose hair is just right and who says "Yes, sir."

John: "Sir, I'd like to begin to live."

Larry: "You look all right to me. Do you go to church? To Sunday School? To prayer meeting?"

John: "Oh, yes, sir."

Larry: "Do you have any non-Christian friends?"

John: "Oh, no, sir."

Larry: "Well, do you date any non-Christian girls?"

John: "Oh, sir. I don't date at all. I'm waiting till marriage."

Larry: "Listen, son . . . you're already *living!* You know what the Christian life is all about!"

I hope this all sounds rather foolish to you. It was supposed to. For living, really living, can't be summed up in the things we don't do, or in all the things we do.

But what kind of life *does* Jesus invite us to

begin to live? What might "beginning to live" mean for you and me?

This question is one people in Jesus' day must have asked too. Jesus didn't keep them in the dark. He gave them a surprising, a jolting, answer.

The Pattern Revealed
Luke 6:20-39

Jesus stood surrounded by a great crowd, eager to touch Him, eager to hear. He began to teach, and though He was speaking to the multitude, He looked steadily at His disciples, for His words would only settle down in the hearts of those who had come to fully trust Him.

His words are some of the most familiar in Scripture. We know them as "the Beatitudes."

Luke 6:20-26

The words seem stark and inexplicable when one first reads them. "Blessed are you poor. Blessed are you that are hungry now. Blessed are you that weep now. Blessed are you when men hate you." And, "Woe to you that are rich. Woe to you that are full now. Woe to you that laugh now. Woe when all men speak well of you" (see vv. 20-26).

The words seem stark, because they seem at first to contrast with the circumstances in which we may find ourselves. And none of us would willingly choose the "blessed" circumstances of poverty, hunger, weeping, and hatred.

To understand Jesus here, we need to realize that the contrast is not between two sets of circumstances but between two ways people react to life in this world. The contrast is between *Jesus' people* and *other people,* and what gives life meaning for them.

We can state quite simply the two principles Jesus communicates in His blessings and woes.

Jesus' people are dissatisfied with what this world has to offer but are happy anyhow. Other people are satisfied with what this world has to offer but are miserable.

We know, for example, that there is nothing wrong with riches in themselves (1 Tim. 6:17-19). So Jesus is not condemning wealth when He pronounces woe on the rich. The Bible tells us that it is a love of money that is a root of every evil (see 1 Tim. 6:10, NASB). In desiring wealth, in fixing one's heart on money, a person opens himself up to woes.

Don was 40 when I met him, a middle-management executive who from college days had determined to work his way to the top of his company and make his million. The week before I spoke in his church, Don had made a discovery that jolted him to the depths of his personality. *He wasn't going to make it!* All that he'd worked for and planned for, all he'd built his life around, was destined to elude him. He was not the "successful and rich" businessman he had pictured himself to be—and he never would be.

At first, Don hadn't known what to do. His whole self-image was shaken. And then, as I was sharing from this very passage of Scripture, Don made a great discovery. The agony he was going through was really God's blessing! God had rescued Don from the misery of becoming the success he had planned to be . . . and, in the process, from seeking to build his life on empty and transient things.

Jesus knew that there is more to life than success, that the meaning of life can't be summed up on a balance sheet or in a bank account. How blessed for Don to weep now, but through the trauma to turn from what this world offers to seek his satisfaction in God. How blessed for Don to be turned, even through pain, toward God's way of living.

It's the same with the other things we set our hearts on. Have you built your life around being accepted by others, being looked to as one of the "in" people? Are you a person who simply has to have everyone say nice things about you—your looks, your clothes, your personality? Jesus said, "How miserable for you when everybody says nice things about you" (see v. 26).

How miserable you must be, to be satisfied with popularity. For you have missed the real meaning of life.

Jesus' beatitudes pierce to the heart of human values, and force us to ask the basic questions that we find so easy to ignore. What is life all about for me? What moves me? What determines my choices? What makes me glad or sad? Am I controlled by my needs, struggling as the pagans do to make sure I have enough and plenty (Matt. 6:25-32)? Am I controlled by pleasure, satisfied with the laughter and distraction I can find in temporary amusements (6:25)? Am I controlled by a desire for wealth, satisfied to see my cash and credit grow (6:24)? Am I controlled by a need to be liked and admired (6:26)?

Jesus says, *"How miserable for you.* You might better be hungry, poor, weeping, and hated. For then at least you might turn from these empty things to Me, to find out what life is really all about."

Jesus' words jolted the men of His day, and they ought to jolt you and me too.

What's your life all about? Are you satisfied that you've found its meaning? Are you ready to listen to what Jesus says about life, and where you can find meaning and purpose? For Jesus, the Lifegiver, knows the meaning of life. And He tells us plainly.

Are you ready to commit yourself to His way?

Luke 6:27-36

Hear Jesus' words.

"I say to all of you who will listen to Me: love your enemies, do good to those who hate you, bless those who curse you, and pray for those who treat you badly" (6:27, 28, PH).

Jesus' answer is simple. *The meaning of life for the believer is to be found in love.* Sold out love.

People, not things, are central in the new life Jesus invites us to begin. Giving, not getting, is what life is all about.

Reciprocity. Sociologists have labeled one kind of human behavior "reciprocity," and noted that in every culture and society the norm, or standard, of reciprocity seems to operate. We have a statement of that norm in the saying, "You scratch my back, and I'll scratch yours." This is all the norm means. You do something good for me; I'll pay you back. You do something bad to me; I'll pay you back for that too!

Most of us are quite bound by this norm. The Joneses sent you a Christmas card last year. So somehow you feel you *have* to send them one this year.

The Carlsons have had you over to their house. Now it's your turn to invite them for dinner—and don't expect them to invite you back until you have.

The norm of reciprocity even operates in the intimacy of family life. You bought me a present? I'll be warm and loving this evening. Your teen-ager mowed the lawn without being asked? Well, sure, you guess he can have the car tonight.

The simple notion that we ought to be nice to those who are nice to us, and are under no obligation to be nice to those who aren't, seems to permeate every human relationship.

There's much to be said for the norm of reciprocity. It helps hold society together. If we couldn't count on people responding in kind, there would be a terrible uncertainty in all our relationships, producing fear and, ultimately, anarchy. So the norm of reciprocity is not bad.

It's just that the norm of reciprocity is not to determine the Christian's behavior! Another norm, another standard, is to replace it in controlling our relationships with other people.

Initiating love. This is the other norm. The Christian is always to take the initiative in loving.

How clearly Jesus says it. "Love your enemies." And, "If you love those who love you, what credit is that to you? . . . Love your enemies, and do good, and lend, expecting nothing in return" (vv. 27-35, NASB). Don't love in the expectation of being paid back, but love because this is a way of life to which you are totally committed as God's child.

It seems like a frightening way to live.

How can I love, knowing I may be hurt by an enemy who may not respond as he should? How can I do good, uncertain about how the other person will see and respond to my actions? It *is* a frightening way to live. Jesus lived this way, and others hated and hurt Him. We may be hurt too. But we will have at least two consolations:

We'll be living Jesus' way.

We'll discover what it means to really be alive; we'll know *abundant* life!

The pattern. As Christians, we're not to model our behavior on the standards of human societies. If we did, we'd look for life's meaning in things, and in the approval of men. If we did, we'd soon fit in and be friendly with our friends, while drawing back from strangers and enemies.

On whom should we model our lives? Jesus tells us. Love, do good, expecting nothing in return, "and you will be the sons of the Most High; for He Himself is kind to ungrateful and evil men. Be merciful, *just as your Father* is merciful" (Luke 6:35, 36, NASB).

My children like a Saturday TV show: "Lance Link, Secret Chimp." It's a spy parody in which chimps are dressed up, flap their lips, and, wearing appropriate clothes, go through motions as someone dubs in dialogue to tell a story. It's so ridiculous to see those hairy, little long-armed creatures dressed up and acting like men.

How startling to realize that God wants no Lance Link sort of life from you and me! He doesn't want us to run around, trying to act like God. The Bible says life for us means to *be like* our heavenly Father! We are His sons, and we are to *be* His sons in this world, moved by His love for even the ungrateful and the selfish, expressing His love in all that we do.

We are to take the initiative. We are to reach

out in love, and break the pattern of the world's reciprocal way of living, that we might express in our personalities the very life of Jesus Christ.

Love. Beginning to live, then, means a new kind of life in Jesus that leads us to truly love people and reach out to them.

Grasping this, each of us is forced to a serious examination of his or her own life.

Do you have others who love you Jesus' way? Others with whom you share; who know your heart, who care? And do you have others whom you love . . . really love, with the involvement, the listening, the total concern that Jesus' kind of love means?

If you are not loved and loving, you haven't yet begun to live.

Not Jesus' life.

Not the new life Jesus died to bring you.

Luke 6:37, 38

If we get the impression from all this that the life of love Jesus proposes is a totally negative experience, with our enemies constantly taking advantage of us, Jesus' next words are encouraging. "The measure you give will be the measure you get back" (see v. 38). The point is clear. In rejecting the norm of reciprocity, you and I are to set a new standard for those around us. In being a model of Jesus' love, we'll find that others do respond to us—and to Him.

An Example to Follow
Luke 6:39-49

Learning. How does a person learn a way of life?

Jesus points out that we learn to live by following a person who knows how to live, and that "everyone, after he has been fully trained will be like his teacher" (v. 40, NASB).

This strikes deep into the hearts of all of us who are parents. How will our children learn to live Jesus' way? Will they see His life in us? Will they grow in Christ as they model their lives after us? Or will they fall far short?

The fact that a way of life is learned by following another person leads Jesus to demand self-examination (v. 42). We have no right to criticize and instruct another on how to live until we've made sure that our own life is in harmony with Christ. If we are blind to God's way of living, and attempt to lead others, both we and they will "fall into the ditch" (v. 39).

The heart. Again Jesus reminds His listeners that the issues of life are settled in the heart. We are not to "act like Christians." We are to be so committed to Jesus Christ and so fully dedicated to His way of life that our actions flow naturally from what we are. "A good tree," Jesus said, "bears good fruit" (see v. 43). When our roots are anchored surely in God's love and our lives are strong with the determination to do His will, our actions will express our transformed character.

Becoming a model. How do you and I become examples of Jesus' life for our children and for the others around us? Jesus gives a simple prescription, one that the whole of Scripture echoes. We are to be people who "hear Jesus' words, and do them" (v. 47). Only in full obedience to the teachings and words of our Lord will we reflect His likeness, and will we be transformed into living examples of His abundant life.

When we live out His words and let God's Spirit work through them in our hearts, then and only then, will we become that vivid example of God's new and different way of life to which we are called.

The Resources to Enable
Luke 7:1-17

Jesus' picture of the believers' way of life given in Luke 6 is the description of a counter-culture. All that He says cuts against the grain of the way men live in our world, and the values most men hold.

Where do we find the resources to enable us to move against the stream, to be really different in spite of all the pressures on us to "fit in"?

Jesus had finished speaking. As He entered Capernaum, the next two recorded events would provide the divine answer to all of us who hear His words with fear.

Luke 7:2-10

The first incident involved a stranger, a Roman army officer who had been posted to occupation duty in the conquered land of Palestine. While in Palestine, this man had come to love the God of Israel and His people (vv. 4-6). He had heard of Jesus, so when a slave of his fell ill, this centurion requested some of the Jewish elders to go and ask Jesus to heal the dying man.

Jesus heard their appeal and turned to follow them. Meanwhile the Roman had had second thoughts. He, a member of the conquering race, realized that he was unworthy of this Man's presence in his home. He sent again, and addressing Jesus as "Lord" (v. 6), asked Him to simply say the word and let his slave be healed, without stooping to enter a Gentile dwelling. "I am a man under authority," the soldier said. As an officer he derived his authority from the whole of the Roman government and power which had commissioned him. Because he spoke with the authority of Rome, he could command his soldiers, and they would obey. "You too," the Roman now said, "are a man under authority." In this admission he gave explicit recognition to the fact that Jesus could speak with the full and complete authority of divine power. All that He might command would be done!

And Jesus "marveled at him, and turned and said to the multitude, . . . I say to you, not even in Israel have I found such great faith" (v. 9, NASB).

This is our first resource.

Faith.

But a particular faith!

Have you realized that the Jesus you know as Saviour has *all power?* That He can command, and His will will be done? If you know Jesus this way, you need not draw back from obeying His words, or launching out on a new life. No, you can obey, filled with the confidence that, separated from us physically as He was separated from the Roman centurion, Jesus yet has but to command, and every need of ours will be met.

We can live God's way if we will.

We can trust Jesus to live His life in us.

Luke 7:11-17

How great is His power? Soon after this, Jesus met

a funeral procession, led by men carrying on a bier the body of a widow's only son. Jesus saw her tears; He cared, and spoke in command: "Young man, arise" (v. 14).

And the dead awoke.

Have you been dead to Jesus' kind of life? Have you lived life the world's way, with your thoughts and desires tangled by the cares that mark the lives of other men, and your love limited to love of those who love you? Then it's time to wake up to what life is all about. It's time to take Jesus' words seriously, to throw off the empty things men set their hearts on. It's time to begin to put into operation His love.

Jesus spoke.

The dead heard His words, and rose to renewed life.

Have you heard what Jesus says to you through Luke?

Then get up!

Let Jesus' power bring you new life—today!

EXPLORE

To further explore this portion of Scripture and its meaning to you . . .

1. Look at what you wrote in answer to "Explore" #4, chapter 1. How would you now change your description of "new life"?
2. Study the Beatitudes (Luke 6:20-26) carefully, placing side by side the "blessed" and "woe" statements. By each couplet, jot down the possible values and life-goals each might imply.
3. Luke 6:27-36 describes Jesus' statement of life's meaning and goal for believers. Read it carefully. Then write down the names of two

friends, and of two others toward whom you feel some hostility or awkwardness.

Now, decide specifically how you might express Jesus' kind of *initiating love* in each of these four relationships.

4. Look over Luke 7:1-17. How many evidences can you find that you can have confidence in Jesus: enough confidence to launch out and live His kind of life?

5. Ask God to help you express and experience His love this week in the relationships you listed in #3, above.

5

Decision

There are some decisions I hate to make.

I particularly dislike deciding what to order from a menu. I'll sit and stare at the listed foods, be the last one to order, and still try frantically to get out of saying to the waitress, "I'll take this."

I had a hard time deciding to buy our last car. I wasn't sure whether it was God's will or my desires that motivated me. And I was very frustrated.

Other decisions—often bigger ones—seem to come easily. It was easy to sign papers to buy our home in Arizona, even though we'd just seen the house. It was even easy to leave my Wheaton teaching position to move out here. It was clearly the right thing to do.

So what can you say about decisions? Some are easy. Some hard. But each of us faces decisions that *have* to be made.

This was the situation in Jesus' day as we come to the events described in Luke 7:18—9:20. Jesus had presented Himself as the Lifegiver and had demonstrated clearly His right to authority. He had openly explained the principles on which the new life He offers is to be built. The counter-culture of love had been sharply defined.

And now people had to choose. They had to decide to trust Jesus and commit themselves to His way—or to reject Him.

What were their reactions under the pressure of imminent decision? Why did those who hesitated hold back? Looking at them we can perhaps understand our own reactions to Jesus' claims. And perhaps we too can see why we *have* to make the choice they tried to avoid.

Why Wait?
Luke 7:18—8:3

There were many who observed all Jesus did and heard all He had said. As Christ drew the issue more and more clearly, all Palestine must have begun to realize that this Man insisted that every person make a choice. One must be for Him or against Him. One must choose Life or Death.

And yet there was hesitancy and doubt. There were deep-seated reasons why even good men drew back and cried out for more time.

Luke 7:18-23

One of those who seemed now to hesitate was John the Baptist! What a surprise to see him waver, for the whole focus of his life had been to prepare the way for Jesus. Still, as we look at the circumstances, we can understand.

John was now in prison (Matt. 11:2), about to be executed by King Herod. The personal pressure he faced must have had something to do with the growth of doubt. But even more serious must have been the fact that Jesus' ministry was not taking the direction John had foreseen. John, like the other godly Jews of his day, was entranced with an Old Testament picture: a vision of a Messianic King who would throw off the pagan yoke and bring in Israel's promised glory days. But he could see no evidence that Jesus was using His miraculous power to strike a blow for freedom. John did not expect the Messiah simply to go around teaching people to love!

So John sent two of his followers to Jesus to question Him: "Are You the One?" (v. 19, NASB). The Bible tells us that "in that same hour, He cured many of their infirmities and plagues, and of evil spirits; and unto many that were blind He gave sight" (v. 21). Turning to John's followers, who had witnessed the healings, He told them to report to John what they had seen.

What had they seen? Miracles? Yes. But *what kind of miracles?* The Old Testament had said of the Messiah that He was "to open blind eyes, to bring out prisoners from the dungeon, and those who dwell in darkness from the prison" (Isa. 42:7, NASB). He would care for those in need. *The Messiah's ministry would focus on people.* So Jesus sent the followers of John back to him to report. Then He turned to the crowds and said, "Happy is the man who never loses his faith in Me" (v. 23, PH).

John hesitated, because Jesus hadn't done what he expected.

What have you expected of Christian faith? Have you seen it as a life of building walls of separation between believers and other people? Or as hiding behind "goodness" to criticize sinners? As rejecting the youth who aches for drugs, or the

adult who curses and tries to hide the emptiness
of his life behind irreverence or pride?

Jesus told John, *Look at Me! See what I do!*
Jesus hid behind no walls. He did not come to
judge. He came to reach out to people, to save,
to heal, to bring hope. To care. And happy are we if
we never take our eyes off Him.

If we look at Jesus, we see *love* at the center of
the life He offers and demands. For people who
expect something different, something less from
faith, no wonder there is hesitancy. But look again
at Jesus. And choose.

Luke 7:24-35

The crowd around Jesus hesitated for a similar
reason to that of John the Baptist.

They had hesitated when John came. Oh, many
had acknowledged God by accepting his baptism.
God had intended all to respond, and offered all
the opportunity to repent. But the leaders, the
experts in Scripture, refused. Many had seen their
action and hesitated too.

Now these same leaders who had criticized John
("Oh, he's too uncouth, too provincial, too fanatic
to pay attention to") were criticizing Jesus, on
contrary grounds ("Oh, He's too smooth—a partying
man, you know, going around and enjoying Himself, and with sinners, too"). These reactions
Jesus labeled childish: like sulky children who
want to play "wedding" when it's time to play
"funeral," and when it's time to play funeral say,
"No—wedding!" John had hesitated because Jesus
was not what he had expected. These others rejected Jesus because they wanted to live by their
own rules.

This is an attitude we have to watch out for. We're too prone to say, "God, I'll let You direct my life, if You give me (1) a wife, (2) a good job, (3) retirement, (4) nice children, (5) no wheelchairs in my future, (6). . . . We hesitate because we want somehow to retain control over our own lives.

But commitment to Jesus Christ involves acknowledging Him as *God!* And to acknowledge Him as God means that He is in control of our lives. He knows best. And we are to follow Him.

Christian faith isn't some game we play by our own rules. Coming to trust Christ means joining ourselves to the ultimate reality: in our union with Jesus Christ we commit ourselves to His rule. And His rule is the rule of love.

Luke 7:36-50

The last hesitation and doubt in this section is seen in a Pharisee, who does not really hesitate; He simply rejects all that Jesus is because he feels, *I have no need.*

The Pharisee. Pharisees were very religious men. We know that they were the conservative believers —not the liberals (who were the Sadducees). Pharisees believed in God, in angels, in resurrection . . . in all the tenets of a conservative biblical faith.

But the Pharisees were *self-righteous.* They made distinctions between themselves and others, saying in effect, "I'm different." They believed that, even in God's sight, they were good.

As Jesus visited in a Pharisee's home, a prostitute (vv. 37, 38) slipped in and began weeping, washing Jesus' feet with her tears. Immediately the self-righteousness of the Pharisee's heart was revealed. "This Man, if He were a prophet," he thought, "would have known who and what manner of woman this is that toucheth Him" (v. 39) . . . and, the implication is clear—"would pull back from her in horror!"

This woman is a sinner.

I'm different.

These two propositions express the basic foundation on which the Pharisee's world ,was based.

She may need cleansing—or better yet punishment.

I'm different. I have no need!

The woman. The woman, who tradition tells us was Mary Magdalene, knew very well that she was a sinner. She came in tears and humbly bowed herself to kiss Jesus' feet.

How did she have the confidence to come? She certainly knew the attitude of the Pharisee . . . his hatred, his contempt. But she must also have known the attitude of Jesus. Clearly she had faith that He would not reject her—not even in the home of the Pharisee.

Jesus. Jesus looked into the heart of each of these two people. In the woman's heart, He saw love and He saw faith (7:47, 50). And in the Pharisee's heart, He saw criticism and unconcern.

"Who loves most?" He asked the Pharisee. "One who is forgiven much . . . or little?" And the answer came. Even the Pharisee supposed that forgiveness and love were linked—the one forgiven much loves much. But one who will not accept forgiveness will never learn to love.

Forgiveness. Of all the figures in the New Testament, the Pharisee is the most tragic. For he alone was totally cut off from Jesus' love; He alone *refused* to respond. And why? Because he kept insisting, "I have no need."

There are things inside each of us that we're ashamed even to think of, that we cringe to imagine another person knowing. Do you realize that Jesus knows? In every detail? And that He loves you still? That He reaches out, now, to forgive?

Forgiveness unlocked a new life for the woman, who had recognized her need and come to Jesus. But refusal to admit need . . . hesitation to take our place before Jesus as sinner . . . cuts us off from Him as surely as it cut off the Pharisee.

Men hesitated and found it hard to decide for three reasons:

•This Jesus isn't what I expected!
•This game isn't played by my rules!
•I have no need; I want no forgiveness!

What reason do you have? Is it as poor a reason as these three . . . poor, because all fail to reckon with the reality that Jesus Christ is God, that He makes the rules, and that each one of us *does* need the forgiveness that ushers in new life?

Respond!
Luke 8:4-55

Decision is essentially response to Jesus Christ and to the Good News He speaks. There will always be varied response from any group of people. But there are important things to remember about whatever response we make.

Luke 8:4-15

The parable of the sower teaches that the Good

News of Jesus falls like seed on men's hearts. As with seeds of grain, God's Word falls on different kinds of ground. Some hear, but quickly are distracted and forget. Some hear with delight, but fall away. Some let the cares and delights of this world choke out God's message of life.

But why did Jesus speak a parable? He explained: "That seeing they might not see, and hearing they might not understand" (v. 10; see Matt. 13:10-14). Jesus had presented Himself and His message in the plainest of words. The seed had been sown. Those who had responded to Him would understand what He said now. Those who refused to respond would soon be unable even to hear.

It seems hard for some to grasp, but it's *true. To hear Jesus' message and to hesitate is to reject.* "Not now" is just as much a "no" as is "never!"

And there comes a time when seeds of truth that have not been allowed to take root are plucked away. *This time had now come in Jesus' ministry.* Men who had seen Him, who had heard His plain words, must now choose. For those who hesitated, and so implicitly refused to recognize the One they were yet unwilling to publicly disclaim, it would soon be too late.

So too for us. Have you seen Jesus? Have you heard His description of new life? Then don't hesitate before Him; the time has come to choose.

Luke 8:16-21

But first Jesus gave further exhortation and example to help men respond to Him with faith. Jesus reminded His hearers how much hinged on their response to Him.

Jesus Himself had stood out like a lamp, shining

clearly where all men could see in Him the light of Life and Truth (v. 16). And again comes the warning: "Take care how you listen . . . whoever does not have, even what he thinks he has shall be taken away from him" (v. 18, NASB). The planted seed, the light of truth, will be removed if it is not used.

And what hinges on response to Christ's message? *Relationship.* "Who is My mother and My brothers? Those who hear the Word of God—and do it" (see v. 21).

Our relationship with God rests squarely on our response to God's message about Jesus Christ. If we hear and believe, we become members of God's family. If we reject, we stay forever outside.

Luke 8:22-55

There's another thing to remember as we ponder our response to Jesus. *Who is it* that we are invited to trust and to obey? Jesus' subsequent actions reinforced the awareness of all around Him as to who He was.

He stilled the sea. Jesus again demonstrated His power over nature, miraculously dispersing a storm and bringing raging waves to a sudden calm (vv. 22-25). The creation obeys the Creator; it knows its God.

He freed the possessed. In Gadara, He was confronted by a man possessed by a legion (at least 6,000) demons, whose bondage was revealed in his filthy nakedness and ferocious strength (vv. 26, 27). Jesus ordered the demons to leave, and freed the man from this supernatural influence. Even the demonic bows before Jesus; Satan knows Him as Lord of all.

He raised the dead. Shortly afterward Jesus was called urgently to attend a dying 12-year-old. Hurrying to her side, Jesus was touched by a woman in the crowd. The woman had been hemorrhaging for a dozen years, yet at His touch was instantly healed. Jesus paused, sought her out, commended her faith, and hurried on. Arriving at the home of Jairus, the girl's father, Jesus found the women wailing and crying in the traditional Hebrew lament for the dead. Turning them all out of the house, He took the hand of the dead child, commanded her to awake, and presented her alive and well to her joyous parents.

The weeping women had seen her dead. They would now see her alive, and spread the word across Jerusalem. There was no need for anyone to know just how He had raised the dead in that closed room. It was enough that all would know she lived.

Even death gives way before Jesus; He is the Lifegiver, and the Lord of Life.

And so, as we think of our response, we too are reminded just who Jesus is. Just who it is that we are invited to believe and to obey. When we see His acts, as the men of that day saw, we know. He is our Lord, and our Almighty God.

Climax
Luke 9:1-20

Then came the climax of the first phase of Christ's ministry. He had presented Himself to men. He had shown them the path of life. What would their answer be? Would they accept Him as their long-awaited Messiah and their King? Or, because He wasn't what they had expected, would they

refuse to admit their need and so reject Him and
His love?

In a flurry of activity, Jesus next sent His disciples
out to go from house to house and village to village
proclaiming His Gospel, healing as He had healed
(vv. 1-6). Even Herod, who had beheaded John,
was perplexed as the reports about Jesus grew and
grew. Could this be John, back from the dead to
haunt him (vv. 7-10)?

When the disciples returned from their mission,
crowds followed Jesus to a plain outside Bethsaida.
He welcomed them, spoke more of the kingdom of
God, and cured those who needed healing. Late
that afternoon Jesus even met their needs for food.
He performed the miracle of the loaves and fishes
(vv. 11-17). These men had now heard His words,
seen His miracles, fed on the bread He had provided.

Finally, Jesus turned to His disciples and asked:
"Who do men say that I am?" (see v. 18)

And the answer came.

"Some say John."

But they do not say, our God.

"Some say Elijah."

But they do not say, our God.

"Some say one of the old prophets."

But they do not say, our God.

"But whom say ye that I am?" Jesus asked the
disciples. Peter answered for them all. "The Christ
of God" (v. 20).

And so it comes down to each of us. Who do you
say that He is? A good man? A religious leader? A
spokesman for goodness and for truth? Only one
answer will do. Only one answer will open the door
to forgiveness and new life.

Jesus is the Christ. He is the Son of God.

And though He was our Lord and God, He would go on to suffer many things, to be rejected officially by the leaders of His people, to be killed, and on the third day rise again—that you and I might find new life in Him.

EXPLORE

To further explore this portion of Scripture and its meaning to you . . .

1. How do you normally respond to the need to make a decision? How might your usual pattern affect your response to Christ, either in becoming a Christian or as a believer?

2. Compare your pattern with the hesitancy of those around Jesus (pp. 61-64). Which are you most like, or least like?

3. Study carefully Luke 8:4-55, and answer the following objections from truths you discover in this passage.

    "I think I'll just wait to decide."

    "I'll listen, but it can't make much difference whatever I decide."

    "I can't be sure Jesus really is God as He claimed to be."

4. Luke 9:18 presents *the* critical question for the individual, to which there can only be two answers: Jesus is the Christ, the Son of God, *or* Jesus is someone else.

    From the study of Luke so far, develop a list of all the evidence you can find that Jesus is, or is not, God's Son.

5. With whom do you now take your stand about Jesus: with the disciples, or with the crowds?

PART II

NEW LIFE FOR US: Jesus' message of new life for believers

6

Be
Disciples

Sometimes the idea of a new life is a hard one for Christians to accept. All too many of us can say, "I became a Christian three years ago . . . or 10 . . . or 20 . . . and I haven't experienced an exciting newness!" For all too many Christians, faith in Christ seems to have meant only settling down deeper into the drab routine of life, comforted perhaps by the realization that there is now hope for a better life after death, but nevertheless despairing of any present sense of meaning and joy. If your experience as a Christian has been like this, how empty the thoughts of the first few chapters of this book must have seemed!

But *receiving* new life from God doesn't automatically bring an experience of that life's fullness. A baby is born into our world. That baby must grow and develop and mature. A full experience of all that it means to be a human being comes only with growth and maturity. It's the same with Christ. Faith is the doorway to a new life. We enter and, still babes, draw our first breath and utter our first cry. *And then all of life opens out before us; then* we *begin* to live. But the full experience of Christ's life, of the meaning and purpose and joy of it, comes to us progressively as we grow.

And now the Gospel of Luke shifts its focus. Christ came, and offered new life to a world that, even after conclusive demonstration of who He was, rejected Him. But some believed. This little band of men who said, "You are the Christ, the Son of God," launched out on new life. From now on, while Christ will talk to the crowds and to their leaders, His message is primarily for those who have life. His message is about discipleship: how His followers can grow into the abundant experience of their new life in Him.

The Meaning of Discipleship
Luke 9:23-26

The second section of Luke is launched with a key passage. The key to the first phase of Christ's ministry was rejection: the key to this second phase is discipleship.

Life saved, or lost (9:24, 25). Any puzzle about Jesus' warning, "Whosoever will save his life shall lose it; but whosoever will lose his life for My sake, the same shall save it" (9:24), is solved when we remember the focus of Luke. As a Christian, with new life from God, you have the potential to be a new and different person. We saw it earlier. Jesus said, "Be like your heavenly Father." God's intention for believers is that we might bear the family resemblance of His Son. You and I are to develop into persons whose character expresses the stamp of God's own heredity. *This is our destiny,* to be like God throughout eternity, and, in this world, to become more and more like Him all the time.

But the potential self (v. 25) can be lost! We can choose to live the old way, by the values and motives that move men in this world. We can live the *old* life, and let the new remain unnourished, buried deep within us. If we do so choose, what we lose is ourselves, our experience on this earth of the person we could have been.

Earlier we saw a great choice each of us must make: Will I accept Jesus' offer of life? Now we see a second choice: Will I be a disciple, put the old behind me, and become new?

This is a question you have to answer. Will you lose your old life, or are you determined to hold tightly to it, and try to save yourself? Or will you let go, turn away from the old for Jesus' sake, and in so doing become the new, the true, you?

Let him deny himself. In verse 23, Jesus gives a profound three-part prescription to anyone who wants to come after Him. The first is: deny yourself.

Self-denial doesn't mean self-rejection. It doesn't mean wallowing in self-loathing, or turning away from everything you enjoy because "if you like it, it must be bad!" The Bible says that God "giveth us richly all things to enjoy" (1 Tim. 6:17). We know that, far from being worthless, you and I are of infinite value. Jesus thought enough of you to die for you. If He loved you so, how can you hate or reject yourself?

But denying self is important in discipleship—as long as we understand that it means *deny everything rooted in the old life.* Deny and reject "the lust of the flesh, and the lust of the eyes, and the pride of life" (1 John 2:16).

Carla had been angry. She struck out at her dad with biting words, then ran to her room. After the flood of tears, she felt better. But she knew too that for her to follow Jesus would now mean going to apologize. How she fought making that apology! She told herself it had been his fault—and in some ways it was. She told herself she *couldn't* go and say, "I'm sorry." Not when *he* should by rights apologize to her first! Everything in her struggled against the self-humbling that an apology would mean. And for a long time she stayed in her room, as the tension within her grew.

Finally, Carla got up off her bed and, denying the fears and pride of her old nature, went to do as she knew Jesus wanted.

This is self-denial. And growing in the Christian life demands just this: the brutal setting aside of pride and fear and all the "rights" that the old self demands as its due, to live instead a Jesus kind of life.

Take up his cross (v. 23). Please note. Jesus did not say, "Take up *My* cross." Instead He says to each of us, "Take up *your* cross."

But what is our cross? Some have thought of it as suffering, a reflection of Jesus' agony that fateful crucifixion day. But that was *Jesus'* cross; that was God's unique will for *Him*. More central than the fact of suffering is the fact that the cross was both God's will for Jesus, and the symbol of Christ's full commitment to the Father's will. Jesus said, "I come to do Thy will, O God" (Heb. 10:9), and in Gethsemane, He prayed "Not My will, but Thine" (Luke 22:42).

What is God's unique will for *you?* This is what taking up the cross means: to choose, as Jesus did, to do whatever God wills. This understanding is supported by a little word: "take up your cross *daily*" (see v. 23). Each day, you and I are to decide to do God's will. In this choice we will live as Jesus did, and be His disciples.

Follow Me. The Living Bible renders this beautifully and well: "Keep close to Me."

How can you and I ever reject the old in us, and decide daily to do God's will? By ourselves, we can't. But we have Jesus' invitation: "Keep close to Me." Jesus doesn't invite us to a "by rule" way of life. He invites us to personal relationship. As we keep close to Him, He encourages us and enables us. He provides the power we need to live triumphantly and to grow in that new life within, which, ultimately, is His.

This, then, is both the way and the necessity of discipleship. To be or not to be disciples is the choice we face: on it hinges the finding or losing of our new selves. We can be disciples as we deny the old in us, choose God's will daily, and follow close to Christ.

And how are we to follow Christ?

The rest of Luke shows us the way.

Luke 9:27-37

Too often talk of "taking up the cross" calls up visions of suffering, and we hesitate in understandable fear. But Jesus saw the cross in a clearer light. "For the joy that was set before Him," the Bible says, He "endured the cross" (Heb.12:2).

After Jesus warned His followers of His coming death (9:21, 22), and began to teach them the meaning of discipleship (9:23, 24), He told them that some of them would soon see revealed the kingdom of God (9:27). Then, the text of Luke skips to a time eight days later when that promise was fulfilled.

Jesus, with Peter, James, and John, went off to a hillside to pray. While praying, Jesus was transfigured. His whole appearance changed. His face and clothing shone. As Moses and Elijah joined Him, all three flashed in heavenly splendor. They talked about Jesus' coming death, and as they spoke the three disciples struggled out of sleep—and saw the glory.

How vital when we draw back from the cross to remember the glory. For us, as for Jesus, a selfless life may lead to discomfort. But the road does not *end* there! The road of self-denial and the daily cross leads surely to the heavenly splendor. And sometimes—often—our life of discipleship provides a taste of glory now.

The three disciples saw Jesus and His glory, and then they heard God's voice from heaven. Totally awed, they fell silent as the divine voice spoke: "This is My beloved Son: hear Him" (v. 35).

Hear Him we must.

If you and I hesitate and draw back from discipleship, let's remember the transfigured Christ. It is God who speaks to us. It is God who shows us the way to life. It is God who commands, and who invites. Let us go on with Him. Let's be disciples!

Survey of the Discipled Life

We now move on to Luke's description of another flurry of activity. Yet in each incident, we see a little more of what it means to be a disciple. Later in Luke we will see some of these themes developed in great detail. Now we see the critical issues in quick survey.

Luke 9:37-43

Trust. The very next day an incident occurred
that showed the danger of misplaced faith. A man
brought his only son to the disciples for healing.
And why not? They were associated with Jesus.
They had recently been sent by Him on a healing
mission. Yet when the disciples attempted to cast
out the spirit that was cause of the sickness, they
could not.

When Jesus came, the man asked Jesus to look
at the boy (v. 38). He had earlier asked the disciples to heal. Now, discouraged, he only asks
Jesus to look! The failure of the disciples had
undermined the confidence of the man in the
Master.

Jesus responded almost bitterly. "O faithless
and perverse generation. How long must I put
up with you" (see v. 41). And then He added,
"Bring Him to Me."

Do we ask from men what we ought to be asking
from God? Have we realized that the "mighty
power of God" (v. 43) is sourced in Jesus alone?
and that all our efforts are futile apart from Him?
The disciple is not a person who acts on his own.
The disciple is a person whose trust is fixed in
Jesus, and whose response to every need is to bring
it to Jesus. In Jesus is found the mighty power of
God.

Luke 9:43-45

Suffering. Immediately after this demonstration of
power, Jesus told His disciples that He would be
handed over to men for suffering and death. This
involved no buffeting by a cruel fate. This was by
Jesus' own choice.

Sometimes we suffer too. How good to realize that, as Christ's disciples, we are not being tossed on waves of circumstance. Even as Jesus' suffering was purposive, so is all that we experience in following Him. God will use our experiences for the blessing of others and ultimately for His—and our—glory.

Luke 9:46-50

Humility. The Twelve were eager for the glory that discipleship would bring. So eager that each one wanted to be greater than the other! Jesus knew what they were thinking, and that it was rooted in the old self, not the new. He took a child, and told them that, at heart, greatness was to care about the little ones, the seemingly unimportant, the individual.

John quickly changed the subject. He was far more at home struggling with a knotty theological problem. He didn't want to talk about caring for a single child. But Jesus' words stood—and still stand. The great among His disciples are those who, like Him, welcome the least, and humbly stoop to care.

Luke 9:51-56

Purpose. One day on a trip through Samaria, Jesus was refused entrance to one village because He journeyed toward Jerusalem. James and John in hot anger asked the Lord to destroy the town with fire from heaven.

Jesus sharply rebuked them. How far they were from His spirit (v. 55). "The Son of man is not come to destroy men's lives, but to save them"

(v. 56). And so, too, the disciple who would follow His Lord. We have a goal in life, a purpose that gives us meaning. Like Jesus, our heart's desire is to save.

Luke 9:57-62

Commitment. Many in Jesus' day volunteered or were called to discipleship. But many fell short of commitment.

There was the *eager disciple* (v. 57) who volunteered to follow Jesus anywhere—until Jesus warned Him that discipleship might lead to discomfort. There was the *reluctant disciple* (v. 59) who, when commanded to follow, wanted to wait until his father had died and been buried. Jesus rejected the excuse. "Go and preach the kingdom of God," He said. But there is no evidence the reluctant disciple obeyed.

There was the *someday disciple* (v. 61), who only wanted a little time. Just to say good-bye to the home folks. Then, someday soon, he would follow. But to Jesus this was unsatisfactory.

What Jesus seeks is the *now* disciple (v. 62), the man who will put his hand to the plow and, without looking back, move straight out to do God's will.

The figure of the plowman is succinct. As a teen, I plowed with an old one-horse hand plow, settling the reins around my shoulders, grasping the handles firmly, struggling to hold the blade level and steady, to make an even furrow. As the first furrow was cut into the virgin ground, I picked out a mark at the far end of the field to fix my eyes on. If I looked back, the plow wandered, the furrow snaking off across the field.

Only by always looking ahead, with eyes fixed on the mark, could I do my job.

This is what Jesus asks of us. To fix our eyes ahead, on Him, and not look back. To take the plow, *now*, and commit ourselves to His task.

Luke 10:1-20

Involvement. Then Jesus sent His disciples out again: 70 sent two by two across the land. Discipleship means involvement in Jesus' ministry of harvest, gathering in all that God has prepared to respond to His message.

And what an involvement! We're involved in Jesus' own ministry. He is Lord of the harvest (v. 2). We're involved in Jesus' way of ministering: going as sheep among wolves, depending neither on wealth or status for our hearing (vv. 3-7). We're involved with Jesus' impact: God's power operates through us as we do His will, whether to heal or to bring judgment on those who reject (vv. 9-16). And yes, we're involved in Jesus' joy: we have a sure relationship with God, and call men to share our fellowship with Him (vv. 17-20).

Luke 10:22-24

Prayer. This last sign of discipleship clearly marked our Lord. He acted in dependence on the Father. He shared His joy with the Father too. And in this prayer He said, "All things are delivered to Me of My Father" (v. 22).

Do you see it?

Do you hear?

Jesus has all power; it is all in His hands. We can come to Him, and in full dependence commit ourselves and our need and our very lives as disciples to His keeping. Then we can step out with confidence to live.

"Blessed are the eyes which see the things that ye see," Jesus told the men who served Him (v. 23). And we're blessed too, if only we see. And if, seeing, we decide.

I'll be a disciple.

I'll learn to live.

EXPLORE

To further explore this portion of Scripture and its meaning to you . . .

1. Look at the illustration of Carla (pp. 75, 76). Can you think of other examples of denying self that are like this? Try to list several from your own experience.

2. Read Luke 9:35, 36 carefully, putting yourself in the place of the disciples. How did they react to what they saw? How do you think you would have reacted? Why?

3. From the seven characteristics of the discipled life (pp. 79-83) select *one* that you feel is most difficult for you. Study carefully the passage of Scripture related to it. You may also use a concordance to look up the theme ("trust," or "prayer," or whatever).

   After your study, record what you have learned and particularly how anything you have learned may help you step out as a disciple.

4. Look at the four kinds of disciples described on page 81 (Luke 9:57-62). Do a character analysis of each. That is, jot down everything that each response seems to you to suggest

about the kind of person who makes it.

For instance, the *now* disciple might be characterized as resolute, determined, excited.

When done, make an analysis of your own character, as you understand it.

5. Jesus claims to have all power. What could He have done for the reluctant disciples if they had only trusted Him enough to obey?

Go back over the character analysis above, asking yourself, "What does Jesus want to do in *this* person, that he might be a real disciple?" Do the same with your own self-analysis. What will Jesus do for you if you let Him?

7

Dead
End

When I was 19, after two years of college, I joined the Navy. At Great Lakes Naval Training Station, I sat in a barber chair and became a "skinhead," was issued my uniforms, and suddenly was introduced to navy life.

There, too, I received some of the traditional misdirection given newcomers in any special group. Left-handed wrenches and lost firing lines and toothbrushes to scrub cracks in the barracks floor were just some of the things I was told to fetch. And, because at first I didn't really know what was expected in this strange new life, I was often confused enough to follow false trails. It was all so new. And I wanted to do the right thing.

In many ways it's the same for us as Christians. To become a believer is to launch out toward a unique destiny: to become more and more like God the Father as the new life He has planted in us grows and matures. We are to learn to think and feel and *be* like Him.

This godly way of life we're to learn is distinctly different from the ways we've known. It's far more than mere morality; it's transformation. So it's easy to become confused about the road to personal renewal. It's easy to wander away from God's pathway onto side tracks that look promising but are really only dead ends.

Luke 10 shows how Jesus began to train His followers in discipleship. He began to show them how to live a new life. His words and actions draw contrasts between the way men of the world live and the way His followers are to live. All that happened, as recorded in Luke, reveals both the straight and narrow way of discipleship, and the dangerous detours that lead us away from our new life's goal.

What are the false trails down which Christians wander? Have disappointments in your Christian life come because you've wandered down one or more of them? In this chapter, we'll look at two false paths which have caused many believers to stray from the path of greatest growth in Christ.

Activism
Luke 10:25—11:13

One of the most deeply ingrained of human notions is that a person must do something to merit God's favor. We accept gifts from other people. But we seem to want to say of anything we receive from God, "I earned it."

Luke 10:25-37

This activist approach to life is implicit in a question put to Jesus by an "expert in the Law (or Scriptures)."

A test. It's instructive to note first that the man

who portrays the activist attitude put an insincere question to Jesus. He asked, "What shall I do to inherit eternal life?" (v. 25) But he wasn't really concerned about Jesus' answer. He wasn't motivated to ask by a personal sense of need; he was trying to trap Jesus. If he had been motivated by honest desire, the answer Jesus gave might have been more direct. As it is, the answer came all too clear. So clear that the questioner soon realized that *he*, not Jesus, was trapped.

"What shall I do to inherit eternal life?" The query itself contains a contradiction. What does anyone *do* to *inherit?* Why, nothing! An inheritance is something someone else has earned. An inheritance comes as a gift. If your father is a millionaire and makes out a will leaving all to you, what did you do to inherit? Why, you were born in his family. The inheritance is based on relationship, not on performance. You do not *do* to *inherit.*

When Jesus turned the question back on the asker, the man answered correctly. The heart of the Old Testament Law, and of all that God seeks to do in the human heart, is total commitment in love for God and love for neighbor (v. 27). The specific commands of the Word can be summed up as love, for a person who loves fully and rightly will do what God's Word reveals to be the loving and the right thing (see Romans 13:8-10). This, then, is at once the simplest and the most profound demand.

Phillips translates Jesus' reply: "Quite right. Do all that and you will live" (v. 27). *Do all that.* Put all of self behind; love God purely and perfectly; love others as you love yourself. *Do all that* and you will live.

These words sounded doom to the questioner.

He had been convicted from his own lips. For he, like every person who has ever lived, had fallen short of doing "all that." We have all had selfish thoughts. We have all hurt our neighbors. We have all failed to put God first in everything. Rather than bringing hope, Jesus' demand that a person do "all that" brought dismay.

Self-justification. It is a characteristic of the activist that, while he wants to earn what he gets, he wants to use balancing scales to determine value. He wants to weigh his good against his bad, hoping there will be more on the "good" side. Jesus' reply said in effect, "All right. Use your balancing scales. But remember that your good actions are not weighed against your bad. They're weighed against the standards of perfection, against doing *all* that love demands."

Realizing that he stood self-condemned, the expert in Scripture tried to justify himself. "Who is my neighbor?" (v. 29). How quickly we all do this! When we realize God's standards are an expression of His own character and are far beyond our capabilities, we try to whittle those standards down to our size. We set up our own little categories for measuring spiritual accomplishment, and so avoid God's clear requirement of total concern and love.

I've recently been visiting a 19-year-old in a Phoenix hospital, a boy who shot himself with a rifle. He went to church when he was a child but finally left as a young teen. He said that the thing that finally earned him his invitation to leave the church was his question: "Why, when you're so proud of sending money overseas for missionaries, won't you have anything to do with the hippies across the street?"

I'm not blaming this church for my young

friend's drift to drugs at 13 and his choice of bad company. But I do wonder. How many of the things we're proud of—our missionary budgets, our separation, our doings and duties—are really expressions of an attempt to whittle down God's standard of perfect love to lists of things we can achieve and perhaps an attempt to feel some pride?

"Who is my neighbor?" In response Jesus told the familiar story of the Good Samaritan. We all know it, and how the injured Israelite lay in pain as first the priest and then the Levite (men who knew and took pride in the Law) passed by. And finally a Samaritan, a foreigner and a hereditary enemy of the Jews, risked stopping to help the injured man. He carried him to an inn and there paid all the cost of his care. Turning to the man who sought to justify himself, Jesus said, "You go, and do likewise."

And here we hear echoes of the Beatitudes and the message that followed: love. Love your enemies. Be like your heavenly Father.

Need. The expert in the Law had come in pride, trying to trap the Lord. Now he went away, and we can hope he went away feeling a personal sense of need. For Jesus challenged this activist on his own field of honor: "go and *do*." Go and *try*. *And when you realize that you cannot possibly do all things that are required by the divine law of love, then perhaps you'll realize that relationship with God cannot be based on human works or accomplishments.* Then perhaps this man would remember the message Jesus had so often taught: life with God starts with confession and forgiveness. Life with God begins when we abandon works and throw ourselves on the overflowing mercies of our God.

Luke 10:38-42

Is the activist attitude found only in the unsaved? Tragically, we find it in the life of real Christians too. It was in Martha's life, and she and her sister, Mary, were very close to Jesus. Martha hurried and bustled and worked and tried to serve Jesus, and became upset when Mary didn't throw herself into the same labors. Jesus had to rebuke her when she asked Him to set Mary to work too. "Mary hath chosen that good part" (v. 42). Mary was sitting, listening to Him.

Luke 11:1-4

Activism is an attitude, an approach to life and to relationship with God. The activist wants to put his relationship with God on a "pay as you go" basis. He feels a tremendous need to do something to earn whatever he receives from the Lord.

In unbelievers this attitude is focused on salvation. "Salvation can't be a gift! Let me do something to win God's approval. Let me earn my way to heaven." Like the lawyer to whom Jesus spoke, such people have not realized that they're lost.

Activism also characterizes the life of many Christians. They too want to live on a pay as you go basis. They feel they have to work to keep God's favor. But we believers are children of the heavenly Father! Helpless children, infants, unable in ourselves to love or to do anything (see John 15:5). Activism—working to earn spiritual gifts and growth—leads only to the frustration that Martha felt as she bustled and hurried—and saw that her sister was closer than she to Jesus.

Then what is God's alternative? If we aren't to grow by self-effort, how do we grow? Jesus' answer comes as we see Him help the disciples develop an attitude, not of activism, but of dependence.

Look at the implications of the prayer that Jesus teaches His disciples now.

Father in heaven,
Holy is Your name.
Your kingdom come.
Your will be done on earth just
    as it is being done in heaven.
Give us our daily bread.
Forgive our sins, as we also
    live forgiveness with others.
And lead us, Father . . .
    not into temptation,
    but deliver us from evil.

                    Luke 11:1-4
                    (Author's paraphrase.)

In this simple prayer, Jesus teaches all disciples to come to God as Father, not as employer. To honor Him, not repay Him. To make request of Him, not to demand what has been earned. To realize our need for constant forgiveness, not to shout in pride, "See how great I'm doing!" To request deliverance, not to promise, "I'll try harder."

The activist attitude is based on the idea that one can do something *for God*. The disciple attitude is based on the awareness that *God can do something* in us!

Luke 11:5-13

The next teachings of our Lord reinforce all that the disciple's prayer implies.

The persistent friend (11:5-10). The first story teaches by contrast. If you have a friend who is at first unwilling to help you, keep at him. He'll finally come down and help just to be rid of you! *Listen,* Jesus says in this story. "Ask, and it shall be given . . . everyone who asks receives." (vv. 9, 10, NASB). *God is not like an irritable acquaintance!* God cares. Ask Him, and He'll give.

The fact of Fatherhood (11:11-13). How do we explain God's eagerness to meet our every need and grant our requests? He is our Father. The key to our attitude and to His goes back again to relationship.

The disciple comes to His heavenly Father, as Jesus did. And God works in his life.

This short section of Luke 10 and 11, then, says something basic to each of us about how we move on in discipleship and grow to be like God. We cannot grow by attempting to earn. Prayer, not performance, is the heart of our new life. It's in depending, not doing.

God the Father is eager to see us grow as His sons. When we come to Him, depending on Him to work in our lives and through our actions, asking Him for His supply, His forgiveness, His leading, His enablement . . . *then* God works His sweeping change in our personalities.

Have you grasped the meaning of your relationship to God? To a doer, God is at best a Friend, who may or may not help, but whose help seems to depend on his own persistent efforts. To the child, God is a Father, on whom he depends totally. "Be ye therefore followers of God as dear children" (Eph. 5:1).

Do you depend on God? Have you come to Him, listened to His Word, and simply asked, "Father, make this real in me"? The road of the activist is a tragic dead end. The highway to transformation is the pathway of total dependence.

Indecision
Luke 11:14-31

The people around saw all that Jesus did in dependence on His Father—but still they hesitated. And
lost the opportunity for new life.

Luke 11:14-23

When Jesus cast out demons, people tried to explain it. It could be by the power of God. But
might there be some other explanation? Jesus'
enemies said His power over demons came from
the prince of demons; it was just a trick to fool
people into trusting Jesus. Christ's answers (vv. 17,
18, 21, 22) were unable to move them. Finally
Jesus faced them simply: "He that is not with Me
is against Me" (v. 23). The time for indecision was
past. People had to choose.

Indecision can spoil the believer's life too. Coming to Christ as Saviour is only the beginning. One
must own Him as Lord and decide for discipleship.
But so many of us hold back! And later discover
that we've wandered into an empty life.

Luke 11:24-26

Jesus illustrated the emptiness of the man who is
forgiven but will not commit himself to God. He
spoke of an unclean spirit cast out of a man. The
man was cleansed, freed from the old dominion.
But his personality, though put in order, was not
occupied! He was like an empty room. What will
happen to him? Other spirits even worse than the
one cast out will come and fill the empty spaces.

Even the believer has no defense against evil so
long as his life is empty. We need the positive,

dynamic presence of Jesus Christ. We must invite Him to fill us and possess us totally if life is going to change. Faith not followed up by total commitment is another tragic dead end for Christians.

Luke 11:27, 28

How do we go about filling our lives with Jesus? Christ said it: "Blessed are they that hear the Word of God and keep it" (v. 28). *This* doing isn't to be confused with the activist's self-effort. Instead, it is an opening up of our life to God, a dependence on Christ for enablement that frees us to respond to God's revealed will. This doing is a response made simply because we want to follow Jesus, and stay close to Him.

Luke 11:29-32

The section closes with words of judgment. The people of Jesus' day had heard Him. Except for a small band, they had hesitated far too long. Now the time of invitation was almost past; the next great evidence of who Jesus is would come in His resurrection (vv. 29, 30).

Then Jesus reviewed for them how great a sin their failure to decide was. When Jonah came to Nineveh, the people of that pagan city had responded with faith. Sheba came to Solomon because she had believed the stories of his wisdom. Yet when Jesus—far greater than any and all the Old Testament figures—had come to His people, had they heard? Had they listened? No, they had hesitated, undecided. And they hesitate still, as the last opportunity of the nation to receive new life from their King now slipped away.

What a lesson for you and me! Have we hesitated too long? Have we drawn back from full commitment to Christ as Lord?

Then let's remember.

Jesus is greater than all.

And it's Jesus, the One with all power, who has said to us, "Follow Me." We can't afford to hesitate. Hesitation has such a terrible cost. We might lose ourselves, and never know in this world all that it means to be transformed.

How good to know that we need not hesitate. For discipleship is no "try harder" life that we're afraid to try because we're sure we'll fail. Discipleship is depending on God our Father, confident in that intimate relationship that as we commit ourselves to do His will He'll give the enablement and transformation that He has promised.

Can you be a disciple?

You can depend on it!

You can depend on *Him.*

EXPLORE

To further explore this portion of Scripture and its meaning to you . . .

1. Look over Luke 10:25-37 again. Make a list of things believers or unbelievers do to try to earn God's favor. Then measure each against the standard of love.
2. Study the Lord's Prayer (really the Disciple's Prayer), Luke 11:1-4. What does it teach about the following: relationship, will, dependence, openness, godlikeness?
3. From your study of these chapters, *define* and *give two illustrations* of "dependence." Then try to explain how a particular action might be

sourced in either a *dependent* attitude or an *activist* attitude, and what difference the attitude would make to God and to the individual.

4. Jot down all the reasons you can think of why a believer might hesitate to commit himself fully to God and to God's will.

5. Read Luke 11:14-31, and from the text attempt to answer each of the reasons you listed for four, above.

8

Illusions

Recently I spoke at a youth conference on evangelism held at Disneyland Hotel in Anaheim, Calif. My wife went with me, and by going early we had two free five-hour periods to spend in the famous amusement park.

An exhibit we enjoyed tremendously was Bell's Circlevision theater in Tomorrowland. By linking nine cameras, the Disney photographers had outdone Cinerama and provided a 360° vision of historic and scenic America, shown on giant screens encircling the watcher. I was particularly jolted when the photographers took us inside a car careening down a twisting San Francisco street—and we actually *felt* the bodily sensations of tipping and turning. It was as if we were in the car instead of standing on the solid carpeted floor inside the theater. Our eyes literally fooled our bodies; we felt what our eyes saw, what seemed to be happening, and not what was actually happening.

The Bible points out a similar phenomenon: "As [a man] thinketh in his heart, so is he" (Prov. 23:7). What a person perceives, what he sees as real, affects his whole personality and behavior.

As Luke moves on in his record of Jesus' training of His disciples, the writer now shows us two particular illusions that can block our progress in godliness. The disciple of Jesus must see life and its meaning as does his Lord. To see as He sees is vital as we seek to *be* as He *is*.

Luke 11:33-36

The lamp. Jesus makes this point in Luke with the illustration of the lamp. "A person puts a lamp on a lampstand so anyone coming in can see the light" (see v. 33).

Picture the lamp of Jesus' day. It was, in all but the wealthiest homes, a shallow dish of olive oil in which floated a wick of flax. The wick was lit, and gave off a flickering light. The lamp was never bright. Coming into a home brightly lit by electricity, we're hardly conscious of the lamps at all. They shed so much light that what we *see* is the room they illuminate. But in Jesus' day men saw the lamp first: they came to the light, and as their eyes became accustomed to the semidarkness, they saw dimly the room that the lamp so imperfectly revealed.

The lamp of Jesus' day, then, was both a focus of attention and illuminator of all that could be seen, however dimly. The lamp would enable a person to pick out the furnishings of a room, and to pick his way through it without stumbling.

The eye (11:34-36). Jesus then pointed out to His hearers that the eye performs a similar function for the body. The eye too is a focal point: on it depends our perception of what surrounds us, and so too the choices that we make. We find our way through this life by evaluating what we see. We make our decisions by what appears to us to be the safest and best way. "When your eye is clear," Jesus then notes, "your whole body also is full of light" (v. 34, NASB). But what if the eye is faulty? What if you don't evaluate correctly? Then you are in darkness! Then you will be unable to move without stumbling. And so Jesus warns, *Watch out that what you mistake as light isn't really darkness!* (v. 35)

With this simple illustration, Jesus has stated a profound truth. If we make a mistake in values, if what we see as important in life is really an illusion, how great is the darkness in which we walk! We will certainly lose our way. We will certainly stumble off the road of the disciple.

What's Important?
Luke 11:37—12:3

Luke records events, after each key teaching of our Lord, which serve to illustrate and demonstrate His meaning. It's the same here. While Jesus was talking about illusory values, a Pharisee (one of those men whose values were completely distorted) invited Jesus to supper. And at that table, Jesus showed a few of the false values against which His disciples must guard.

Luke 11:37-44

The conflict in values appeared as they were seated at the Pharisee's table. The Pharisee noted with surprise that Jesus didn't "wash" before the meal.

The washing here was not for cleansing but as a

ritual. Over the centuries the Pharisees had embellished God's Law with many human traditions. In Jesus' day, these men were careful about every detail of their lives, and their sense of religious superiority was rooted in this care. So before each meal they would carefully wash, dipping their hands into a bowl of water, raising their arms to let the waters run down their elbows. One who had not gone through this ritual washing would not be considered "clean" enough to eat.

Jesus didn't follow this tradition! And noting His host's reaction, Jesus launched into a scathing critique of the Pharisee approach to life and of the values that were at its root.

What were some of the externals that seemed important to the Pharisees? Ritual washing. Ceremonial cleansings of every dish from which he ate. Such careful tithing that they would count the tiny leaves of household cooking herbs to make sure one of every ten was taken to the Temple. "These are the things you have been concerned with," Jesus charged (see v. 42). On such compulsive concern with externals, the Pharisees had built their reputations for holiness! In their pride, they loved to sit in the front seats of the synagogue, and loved to have men bow to them in public recognition of their spiritual superiority (v. 43). And they accepted all this deference as their due. They actually thought they were spiritually superior, because they were so careful in keeping the minutiae of what they felt to be God's Law.

How easy for us to fall into a Pharisee way of life. We too have our traditions, our own criteria of spiritual superiority. How many meetings a week are we careful to attend? How many responsibilities have we accepted? Are we careful to avoid movies at the theater but watch the same movies at home on TV? How many other things do we refrain from legalistically? Then because we *do* read our Bibles 17 minutes a day, or because we *don't* wear lipstick, we walk out proudly to accept the admiration of humble folks who haven't reached the spiritual heights that we've attained!

But are such things measures of spirituality? Are there any externals (the lesser duties that we need not leave undone, v. 42) we ought to be *primarily* concerned with?

Not according to Jesus. As He spoke to the Pharisees and revealed the shallowness of their faith, Jesus showed again what His disciples *are* to value. Cleanse the inner man by doing good (v. 41). Care about people, not things (v. 39). And never lose sight of the justice and the love of God, for these are the things with which we ought to be most concerned (v. 42).

True spirituality is of the heart. It is essentially a heart that beats in harmony with the heart of God. When we truly *care* about the things God cares about . . . about justice and love and doing good to others . . . *then* our eyes are cleared of illusion. Then we see clearly, and then we become free to live as disciples.

Jesus was interrupted by an expert in the Law. But later He returned to His theme. "Watch out for the yeast—that which grows and grows and comes to dominate the whole—the yeast of the Pharisee, which is hypocrisy" (see 12:1).

I used to think that hypocrisy was doing something you knew was wrong to fool others. It can be at times; one meaning of the original word is pretense, play acting. But there is another meaning: "outward show." The Pharisees were not pretending! *They actually thought that the outward show, the ritual, and the attention to minutiae, was the real thing!* They had mistaken externals for the heart of faith.

Because they mistook outward show for reality, their inner eye was blind. What they thought was light was darkness! With their values wrong, all that they might do could only lead them deeper into the dark night of the soul.

Luke 11:45-54

Jesus' listeners understood His blunt words. An expert in the Law, not a Pharisee but one who realized that his approach to religion was very like theirs, objected: "Teacher, when You say this, You insult us too!" (11:45, NASB)

Jesus agreed! And He went on to condemn them openly. In their pride, these men insisted that everyone focus on externals as they did. Rather than attempting to help others know God, these legalists laid more and more requirements on the people. "To please God, you must do this. And this. And that. And the other." In their emphasis on works and self-righteousness, they stole the key to a true knowledge of God: that God can be approached by sinners seeking forgiveness, and that transformation of heart and life follows. The lawyers had rejected this approach to faith. They had never gone in this door, and now they hindered others from entering (v. 52). "Yes," Jesus informed them, "you are worthy successors of fathers who murdered the prophets God sent to them" (see v. 48).

Then Jesus left them. The angered men had again rejected His evaluation. Instead of asking,

Is our light really darkness? their hatred fed on what He said, and grew.

Luke 12:1-3

Later Jesus warned His disciples, and warns us, against coming to view life as did the religious people of His day. Outward show had become more important to them than the heart; the external had become the reality. Yet, in a coming day, no one will be able to hide behind his illusions! "There is nothing covered that shall not be revealed: neither hid, that shall not be known" (v. 2). When God reveals reality, how vital that you and I not have wandered with the Pharisee into an empty and cold world of outward show.

Between Two Worlds
Luke 12:4-48

It's easy for us to fall victim to illusions. Part of the reason is that a disciple lives in two worlds: the material-social world around him, and the invisible, spiritual world operating within and through the visible. Conflicts between these two worlds often occur. A choice that seems wise according to appearances is often not wise at all!

So we seem caught between what we see around us and something that God says is far more real. Standing between the two, the disciple needs to come to the place where he commits himself to one world only. He needs to recognize appearances as mere illusion, and grasp the tremendous fact that what is not apparent to us is far more real.

Carol's mother insisted she work toward a teaching certificate in college, rather than take the training Carol felt she needed for missions. Carol's mother was moved by a concern for her daughter's security; certainly education was the safest course. So it might appear! But appearances can be misleading.

Luke 12:4-12

Jesus began to teach this truth to His disciples with a simple warning. Don't fear (stand in awe) of powers that can kill the physical body. Stand in awe of God, who can give life to or destroy the living personality (see vv. 4, 5).

This instruction might well bring terror, were it not for Jesus' next words. Not a sparrow falls, or a hair of your head, but that God knows. Don't fear; "Ye are of more value than many sparrows" (v. 7). God's tremendous power is used *for* us, not against. He cares. We are important to Him.

How important? Jesus goes on to show that when a person acknowledges Christ, that person is acknowledged by Christ in the presence of the angels. *What happens on earth is important in heaven! The two worlds which seem so separated are actually linked . . . and God is in control of both!* How wonderful to realize that God, who does control, also values us, and cares.

Luke 12:13-21

Hearing Jesus speak of God's control over the material, a man in the crowd shouted out, asking Jesus to make his brother divide an inheritance. This man had completely misunderstood what Jesus was teaching. *This world is not the important one!* So Jesus warns us all. "Note that, and guard against covetousness in every form" (see v. 15).

How quickly we come to think that this world is the important one, that somehow life consists in the abundance of things a person possesses. The rich fool felt he had more than plenty—so much he tore down his barns to build larger ones. He was comforted to think that he had all he would ever need, and told himself, "Soul, you have . . ."

Remember that biblical *soul* is not some part of the personality that breaks off and goes on after death. *Soul* is personality itself. This man was saying, "*Self,* you have plenty." In so doing he confused his life in this world, his body, with *himself!*

But a human being is more than an animal. He is more than a body and bodily awareness. A human, formed in the image of God by His own hand, is a deathless individual who will exist in self-conscious awareness throughout eternity—either with God, or separated from Him.

The rich man thought that this world was all, that life consisted of luxury and plenty. How blind! And how tragic a mistake! That very night, Jesus said, the man's personality was separated from his body, to leave this world and answer to God. And all his *things* would be left behind.

When we see reality clearly, we come to realize both that the material is under God's control, and that the material is irrelevant to the real meaning of man's life.

Luke 12:22-34

Jesus had warned the crowds that abundance and luxury do not hold the meaning of life. Now he adds a word about necessities to the disciples. The disciple is not even to be concerned about food and clothing! His attitude instead is to be one of trust in God, who knows his needs, and who is in control of all.

There are two things that Jesus' words bring to our attention:

(1) Disciples need not live in a state of anxiety. We can trust God for our physical needs as for all else. Because we need not be worried about such things, when we make decisions we're free to choose God's will, even if it involves the loss of all we possess (v. 33).

(2) Our use of material resources may well reflect our commitment to God, and the extent to which our hearts are set on His kingdom and righteousness (v. 31). Jesus said, "Where your treasure is, there will your heart be also" (v. 34). If we treasure things, possessions, or wealth, then our heart will be drawn away from God. Like the rich fool, we will seek meaning in things. And with our vision thus clouded, we'll lose our way as disciples.

Luke 12:35-48

Jesus closes His discussion of the disciple attitude with a warning. Be alert!

Christ's coming seems to many to stretch farther and farther into the future. How easy to settle down in this world! How quickly we, as servants of God, can come to enjoy what He has left in our charge while He's away! Yet we know the Master's plan (v. 47). We know that this present world will be dissolved in fire (2 Peter 3:7-13). We know that all we do should be done in view of the reality of our Lord's appearance. How happy for us if we never let the world around us close our eyes to God! How happy if we resist the constant temptation to build our lives on things rather than on His coming!

There is one other implication of the story of the servant that is important. The servant is responsible *only* to see about his master's business. The master is the one responsible to see the servant's needs are met! If we choose to live as disciples, as God's servants, He Himself accepts responsibility for our care. What better provision could we have than that?

With the confident assurance that God is in charge of the seen as well as the unseen, we can be free both from a desire for luxury and an anxiety about necessities. And we can see clearly the blindness that leads many astray as they seek to live in two worlds.

Closing Doors
Luke 12:51—13:9

The Lord's ministry is now concentrated on instructing His disciples. But the door to life, while swinging shut, is not yet closed to the crowds. And so again urgent warnings come: it is time, *now*, to decide.

Luke 13:51-53

Have you been drawing back from Jesus because you're afraid that a decision for Him might cause conflict? Don't hesitate! Yes, conflict may well come. There may be a division . . . but there *must* be a decision.

Luke 12:54-59

How can people who can judge the weather with a glance toward the sky not interpret the meaning of the times in which they live? There is no time left; the signs have been clearly given. Now all the earth is on its way to court, to appear before the Judge of all. How vital to settle now, out of court, before sentence is passed! Soon it will be too late.

Luke 13:1-5

Still people tried to avoid the issue, to speak of curiosities. And Jesus warned them plainly—the men killed in a recent disaster were no more guilty than they. "Change your outlook, or you will die as tragically" (see v. 5).

Luke 15:6-9

And then He gave them a final parable. The fig tree, representing Israel, had been planted and tended but brought forth no fruit. Now it was given one last chance. Fertilized, dug around to provide extra moisture, it was to be watched. And if it still proved barren, it would be rooted out.

Now the door seems almost closed; only a crack remains. Who will hurry to enter? Who will listen to Jesus' warnings?

And who will listen today? Luke has been speaking to disciples, yes. But he still remembers those who stand outside, too proud or too fearful to come to Jesus for new life. To both disciple and outsider, Luke says, decide.

The door is closing.

The Master of the house draws near.

The judgment or the joy awaits. Which will it be for you?

EXPLORE

To further explore this portion of Scripture and its meaning to you . . .
1. Paraphrase Luke 11:37-44, imagining that Jesus is speaking to present-day Pharisees.
2. From Luke 11:37-54, do an analysis of the chief characteristics of the Pharisee attitude, and an analysis of the contrasting attitude that is to characterize Jesus' disciple.
3. Look at the illustration of Carol and her mother on pages 103-104. What does the teaching of Luke 12:4-48 say to them?
4. If you felt truly free of all concern for necessities or desire for luxuries, how would your life be different than it is now?
5. How does "seek first the kingdom of God" help us put our sense of freedom from concern for things in perspective?

9

Games

Backyard games are great, if . . .

When my oldest boy was about 12 we got a game called Jarts, which consists of big outdoor darts that one tosses at a circle marked out on the ground. We enjoyed the game till it became clear that my son was taking the competition too seriously, becoming frustrated when I got ahead. Finally I got smart and changed the rules. Rather than trying to see who got to 21 first, we began to see how many tosses it would take us to reach a set goal together. And then we began to enjoy the game.

There's something about any win/lose game that has great potential for frustration and even for humiliation. Today, this same son plays basketball with me in our backyard, and enjoys beating me. We play Ping-Pong, and he enjoys trying to win a set number of games each month. He's older now; he can hold his own, or feel good about progress he makes even when he doesn't win. But when win or lose becomes everything, it can be destructive.

Games People Play, by Eric Berne, suggests that we all play games with each other; we all try to win. We manipulate others to gain some temporary advantage, and make them serve our ends or our pride.

We all have a tendency to approach life this way. The desire to win, to feel ourselves "better" than others, or to gain a benefit at someone else's expense is all a part of the distortion sin has stamped in the human personality. It's *natural* to play such interpersonal games, even for the believer. But it is totally contrary to the way of life of the disciple.

Luke illustrates in the experiences and conversations of Jesus some of the strategies that people use to gain advantage. And He shows why these are contradictory to the life of discipleship. In His probing at the inner motives of men, Jesus probes our lives too. He helps us discover hidden patterns in our lives that might hold us and others back from full experience of the disciple's abundant life.

People Are Pawns
Luke 13:10—14:35

This is the chief characteristic of all the games that people play for personal advantage. In these games, people are pawns, pieces on a game board to be used to win a desired end.

Luke 13:10-21

The first game that Jesus confronts is one we've seen before. Its name is *formalism*.

Teaching in a synagogue on the Sabbath, Jesus

saw in the congregation a woman who had been oppressed for 18 years, bent almost double and unable to straighten up. He called out to her and laid hands on her. Immediately freed, she stood upright and praised God. And the president of the synagogue was *annoyed!* In fact, he was so upset that he announced: "There are six days in which men ought to work; in them therefore come and be healed, and not on the Sabbath Day" (v. 14). Immediately, Jesus labeled his response hypocrisy, "outward show." This man was so caught up in the forms and the traditions that he lost sight of people! But the same man would think nothing of untying an ox on the Sabbath and leading it to drink (v. 15).

Jesus' illustration pierced through all the pretense to reveal the utter emptiness of formalism. His words "reduced His opponents to shame" (v. 17, PH.). And then He went on to warn. In the Kingdom, many birds will come to roost on the tree faith produces. Don't mistake them for fruit! In the Kingdom, formalism—the idea that the outward show and form is the reality—can, like yeast hidden in flour, too quickly permeate the whole.

The holy feast of Israel was to be observed with unleavened bread. Christ's followers too are to throw out this leaven of the Pharisees, lest concern without outward show come to dominate the disciple's life.

Luke 13:22-30

The second game Jesus probed is *name dropper.* He warned against people who associated with Him without commitment. The day will come, He

warned, when such people will find themselves
outside. Then they'll call out: "Lord, please open!"
(see v. 25) They'll protest, "Why, we've been at
dinners with You! You've taught among us in our
very streets!" (see v. 26) But He will reject them:
"I do not know where you are from" (v. 27, NASB).
Origin, not association, is what counts! Spend all
the time in church you want. Association with believers won't make you a Christian. You must have
the life that comes from God.

Luke 13:31-35

Then the Pharisees (who hate Jesus, and by now
have been plotting to kill Him), rush up to warn
Him of impending danger (v. 31). And the name
of this game is, *find the weakness.*

The Pharisees didn't care if Herod came to kill
Jesus. They would have been delighted! But the
rumor might help them. Rumors make people
worry. A lie here or there might upset a person
you don't like. It might make him uncertain, or
even produce fear. If such a weakness shows up
in a person's character, you have something to use
against him. You have a prop for your own pride,
ammunition for your smearing remarks. "Did you
hear how Jesus just fell apart when He heard
that . . . ?"

But Jesus wasn't afraid. He knew already far
more than they about His coming suffering, and
He never drew back. But He took no pride in
courage. Instead, His heart was touched with compassion for the very men who hated Him and now
tried to break His spirit. He mourned over a
Jerusalem that had rejected and would crucify
Him, and in turn be destroyed (vv. 34, 35).

Luke 14:1-6

We have a concept in our legal code called *entrapment*. It protects a person from being solicited by law enforcement officers to commit a crime, for which he can then be arrested. Crimes must be committed on the initiation of the criminal, not the police.

But entrapment is one of the games we often play with others. We set up a trap into which we hope they'll fall.

The Pharisees, knowing Jesus had healed on the Sabbath, had him to the home of one of their most respected members (v. 1). Right across the table from Him, they seated a man afflicted with dropsy. And they watched.

Jesus brought the issue into the open. "Is it right to heal on the Sabbath or no?" (see v. 3). Then, when they would not answer, He healed the man and let him go. Again He shamed His critics, pointing out that even a cow fallen into a pit would be lifted out on Sabbath.

It's bad when a game we play (such as *find the weakness*) is designed to embarrass another person. It's far worse when we bring in an innocent third party to use against our foe. How had the dropsyed man felt? Had the Pharisees cared whether he were helped or not? Hardly. He was merely a pawn, a way to get at Jesus. It's true, when we see others as pawns, and struggle for our own advantage, we soon begin to involve and treat bystanders as unfeelingly as did the Pharisees.

Luke 14:7-15

Jesus observed behavior at a feast that revealed another game that pride and selfishness motivate:

spotlight. The point in this game is to make sure that everyone sees and admires you. Jesus saw men competing for better seats at a banquet (seating was ordered in those days with the most important guests ranked nearest the head of the table).

After pointing out the danger of pushing yourself into a high seat (you might be embarrassed if your host reseated you lower!), Jesus noted that the person who is constantly seeking to gain the approval or respect of others by exalting himself will ultimately be humbled.

How empty when we act from motives of "what will others think?" How meaningless the approval of men, when only God can accurately evaluate, and only His approval counts in the long run.

Jesus suggested to His host that he might better invite the poor and the homeless to his banquet —not friends who would repay him in kind. How much better to reach out in love to those whom no one loves but God! We can be assured that God will more than repay acts of love when resurrection comes (v. 14).

Luke 14:15-24

Then, Jesus told a story to those who were too busy with their own concerns to come to the feast of life God has prepared. His teaching was stimulated by a comment: "Blessed is he that shall eat bread in the kingdom of God" (v. 15). Jesus told a story that illustrates basic Gospel truth.

The invitation has been given (v. 16). Many were invited—even the game players, whose emptiness Jesus has now exposed. Yes, even game players are called by Jesus to come to His heavenly celebration;

He came to save all. Yet all began to make excuses (v. 18). Each was too busy with his own affairs: his own profit and gain and pleasure.

The excuses were rejection. For whatever reason a person may excuse his actions, saying no to an invitation is still rejection. A person who fails to respond to Jesus' offer of life has rejected Him. Salvation is a *yes* or *no* kind of thing.

The house will be filled (v. 23). Those who judge themselves too busy or who are too involved in playing their games to respond cannot keep God's house from being filled. The Gospel invitation goes out across the world to all who will receive. How strange that, often, those whom the "best" people reject are the very ones who respond to God!

It will soon be too late (v. 24). Again the words of warning come to Jesus' generation. Though they were invited, those who reject the invitation will be excluded from Christ's great supper.

Luke 14:25-33

Jesus turned to the crowd, which had witnessed His encounter with the Pharisees. They *had* to choose.

Even the closest of human ties that might sway a man against a decisive choice must be set aside. (So the word "hate" in verse 26 makes clear in an idiom men of that day would understand. To "hate" was to decisively reject all other claims to an estate in favor of one named heir.) Jesus said, "Take up the daily cross of God's will for you, and follow Me!" (see v. 27).

For us, Jesus' words and actions speak clearly. We must reject every little game men play for personal advantage. Formalism? Reject empty show and look to the heart, to care about the people Jesus loves. Don't be concerned with appearances; value instead your commitment to the Lord.

Set *all* aside, and choose to live in Jesus' way.

So each following illustration speaks: choose! Count the cost (vv. 28-32). Realize that to reject Jesus is to lose yourself. Therefore, forsake everything to follow Him (v. 33).

The Prize
Luke 15:1-32

What ways of living with others *does* Jesus commend to His disciples? He has decisively rejected playing games that use others as pawns. Instead, Jesus teaches that His disciples are to treat people as the prize!

Luke 15:1-10

The Pharisees, whose cold-hearted formalism never made them hesitate to use others, began to criticize Jesus for His interpersonal relationships. "Why, this Man receives and eats with sinners!" (see v. 2). In response, Jesus told the story which launches the next two chapters of Luke's Gospel, and which clearly reveals the principles that are to guide us as we live with others.

If a man with a hundred sheep loses one (vv. 4-7), he will search for it, and rejoice when he finds it. If a woman loses one coin (vv. 8, 9), she'll sweep and hunt through the whole house. When she finds it, she'll rejoice. It's the same for God with people. "There is joy in the presence of the angels of God over one sinner that repenteth" (v.

10). *To God, people are a prize.* We are important and valued, and the transformation of a single sinner brings joy not only to God but also to all who share His heart of love.

Have you grasped what this means? God won't manipulate you or play games with you. You're not a pawn, not even in His age-long battle with Satan. No, you are instead a shepherd's lost lamb, a woman's lost dowry coin. God the Father *loves* you. And all He does with you will be for your benefit and good.

What a wonderful confidence this is! I am not used by God to gain some mysterious end of His; I *am* the end, the goal, that in me all His love might be expressed, and that I might thus share His glory.

Luke 15:11-32

How appropriate that the story of the prodigal son follows Jesus' assertion of God's love. Does God really love us? We've rejected Him, wandered in far countries, spent the good gifts He's given in selfish and often sinful pursuits. What's His attitude toward us now? God is watching for us, always (v. 20). When we turn to Him, He runs to greet us. Stilling our confession, He assures us of His changeless love. And He prepares the abundant life for us: the fatted calf of transformation.

But there was an older son, who represents the Pharisees standing by. This man was unmoved by his brother's return. He was angry, and criticized the father (vv. 25-30). In his anger, the elder brother refused the love the father offered *him*— even though the father himself went out to entreat the angry son to come to the feast (v. 28).

Whose character do we bear? The father's, whose love overcame and made a way for the dead to live again? Or the elder son's, whose anger at love and at forgiveness so blinded him that he could not even see that *he* needed forgiveness too? How exciting that when we have experienced our Father's love, we are invited to be like Him, freed forever from that cold self-centeredness that cuts us off from one another, and from God!

Luke 16:1-13

The Pharisees had turned life upside down. They used people to gain things. Now Jesus set the values aright, and pointed up the worth of individuals to a loving God. He showed that the servant of God the Father must also use things to gain the good of men and women.

This is the point of the story of the unjust steward. He was commended because he was wise in using things to gain his ends. Jesus' point is clear. We too are to determine what is to be *used* and what is to be *gained*, and then be faithful in our commitment to the truth that persons are of greater value. No one can serve two masters. We will either be mastered by our love for persons, and give of what we own to meet their needs, or we will be mastered by our love for things, and in the end use people to gain them (v. 13).

The Pharisees heard what He said. They scorned Him, because at heart they were lovers of money (v. 14).

What's *your* reaction to this teaching of Jesus? Do you feel a desire to excuse or explain away the obvious demand? If so, perhaps you've wandered from Christ's commitment to the value of persons, and begun to value things over the hearts and lives of men.

The Law and the Heart
Luke 16:15-31

Once again, Jesus openly attacked the Pharisees: "You advertise your goodness before men. But God knows your heart. And all that you hold splendid is to Him utterly detestable (see v. 15).

Luke 16:16, 17

And then Jesus turned to speak of Law. Why of the Law? Because it is in the Law that these hard men rooted all their pride. Yet, Law as well as Gospel proclaims the love of God. No one can read passages like the first chapters of Deuteronomy, or the Prophet Isaiah, and be unaware that God is concerned about men, that His every word is spoken in love.

The Law, an expression of the way that men might live love with one another, will not pass away. The Law, in which the Pharisee's sourced their pride, condemned them, for they had not responded to its central message: "Love God. Love your neighbor."

Luke 16:18

Why the seemingly out-of-place reference here to divorce? Perhaps as a reflection of the readiness of the Pharisee to use others, even to multiplying grounds for divorce. If we truly care about the welfare of our husbands or wives, how many of us would ever come to even consideration of divorce?

Luke 16:19-31

This segment closes with the story of the rich man and Lazarus. It is probably a true story, about real people. Scripture nearly always clearly marks off His parables and illustrations, and no parable uses an individual's name.

This story focuses attention on a man who seems to have summed up life in things. He was rich; yet no love for his fellowman moved him to use even a little for the beggar Lazarus.

When death came, the man left his riches behind. With all illusions and false appearances stripped away from reality, he entered the torments of an eternity for which he had not prepared. *What a demonstration of the truth contained in the Beatitudes!* The one who was rich, who laughed then, suddenly discovered that his destiny was filled with woe. And Lazarus, one of the blessed poor who must have sought the meaning of life in God, received eternity's good (v. 25).

Jesus tells of a conversation in the afterworld. The rich man looked across the gulf fixed between blessedness and woe and saw Abraham (the father of those who believe) with Lazarus. He called for aid. But it was too late.

Then came an unusual request. If only Lazarus could be sent to the earthly home of the man now in torment, to warn his five brothers who were still living. Certainly they would listen if a familiar man returned from the dead to speak with them. Certainly then they would repent and change the whole direction of their lives.

Abraham's answer must have jolted. "They have Moses and the prophets" (v. 29). They already had the Word of God, that Word in which even Law breathes love. If they had not listened, if they have not confessed and sought forgiveness and a new direction for life in response to God's Word, even resurrection will not move them.

And, we know from history, resurrection *did not* move them. The Man who spoke these very words to Pharisees and crowd was soon to die, and then to be proved victor over death, raised by the Father's power. Still many would not believe.

Has God's Word touched you?

Have you listened to the clear call of love? Having turned to Christ, have you cast all else behind? Are you *fully* committed to the disciple trail?

How rich a life this life of love is! This life to which Jesus calls.

EXPLORE

To further explore this portion of Scripture and its meaning to you . . .

1. Think of all the people with whom you have some regular relationship. If they ever give the impression of trying to use you, jot down how. Do you ever try to use them? Why? How?

2. Jesus exposed several games that people play to gain personal advantage over or through others. Look at each of the games discussed in the first section of this chapter, and the passages of Scripure in which they are described. For each, try to set up the rules of the game; that is, how it's played.

For example, one game is "formalism." Some rules of that game might be:

A. Set standards narrower and higher than most people can keep.

B. Be sure to sneer a little when someone falls short.

C. Keep insisting people's problems are less important than "doing things the right way."

You can add more rules to this list for the game of formalism, and make up lists for each of the other games as well.

3. Imagine you were asked to write a short TV script to present in modern form the story of the prodigal. What would each of the three central characters do and be? How would the various stages of the prodigal's alienation be described in contemporary terms? (Luke 15: 11-32).

4. What is it like after death? Does a person just become nothing, or a "spirit," or what? Study carefully Luke 16:19-31, and develop from it a description of life after death.

5. Pawn or prize. What is *your* basic attitude toward others? Reread Luke 15 and 16, asking God to help you see how to show love to all with whom you come in contact.

10

Only Believe?

We've all seen a child seated in complete concentration, taking apart a new toy. Somehow it seems so important to find out just how something new works.

We may feel the same way about "faith." What does it mean to "believe"? Does it mean sitting back and waiting for God to do something? Or does it mean acting? And how can I tell if my actions are just self-effort, that *activism* that is to be no part of the disciple life?

Questions like these plague many Christians, many who set out to be disciples but hesitate at times, uncertain how to proceed.

Jesus' first disciples were uncertain too. The Lord taught them the functions of faith. We are taught the same through the record in Luke 17:1—19:11.

The Problem Posed
Luke 17:1-10

One day the question of faith crept unexpectedly into a conversation between Jesus and the Twelve.

124

He was speaking a word of woe about those who put temptations to sin in others' way, to cause them to stumble (vv. 1, 2). This word was not only to outsiders; the warning is needed by disciples too. Too often our ways of living with others harm rather than help!

Jesus became very specific. "If your brother sins, rebuke him; and if he repents, forgive him" (v. 3, NASB). This is doubly hard. It's much easier to keep still when someone sins against us, and to try to hide the pain. We sometimes even think we're being "spiritual" by trying to ignore the wrong. But failure to be honest, trying to give the "outward show" of nothing wrong when there *is* something wrong, isn't God's way. "Speak the truth to one another," (see Eph. 4:15), the Bible teaches, "in love." Real love speaks out to remove the barrier that even inadvertent sins erect. The loving thing to do is to rebuke the person who sins against you, for he needs the cleansing that forgiveness can bring as much as you need the barrier of hurt removed. So Jesus says, "rebuke him."

And if he repents? Forgive! And this is difficult too. For our old self dwells on slights and hurts and takes a perverse pleasure in self-pity and "righteous indignation."

But Jesus made it even more difficult. "If he sins against you seven times a day, and returns to you seven times saying, 'I repent,' forgive him" (v. 4, NASB). The disciples were upset at this. "Lord," they cried, "increase our faith!" (v. 5).

I can understand their feelings. "Lord, that's *hard*. We need more faith if we're to be able to do something like *that*!"

When first married, my wife and I lived in a house trailer 35' x 8'. Our living room was only about six feet wide. And I had a problem. Ever since my teen years, I've been driven up the wall by mouth noises—especially gum, chewed with open-mouthed vigor. And my new wife was a gum chewer! As I'd sit at the table, way across our six-foot living room from my wife, I'd become aware of a growing, echoing sound: ker-chump. ker-chump. KER-chump. KER-CHUMP!

Finally, in desperation, I'd mention the gum noise, and be given a quick, full-hearted apology. And there'd be silence, as gum and mouth were clamped carefully shut. For a while. But soon, engrossed in reading, she'd forget. And then the sound would reach me again. And grow. Until I just couldn't stand it any longer, and in desperation would speak again. She was always quick to say, "I'm sorry." But after several recurrences, I'd begin to wonder, and to feel upset. "She *couldn't* care! Not and do it *again*!"

No wonder the apostles cried out to Jesus, "Help! If we have to live like *that* with people, then, Lord, increase our faith!"

But how can we understand Jesus' answer? He hardly seems to sympathize. "Faith?" He seems to pass over their request. "A tiny grain of faith will move this tree and plant it in the sea" (see v. 6). The important thing to note here is that Jesus was no speaking to Pharisees, who had no faith. He was speaking to the Twelve, who *did* believe, and *who did have faith*!

Jesus' next words explain His reaction. He spoke to them about a servant—literally, a bond slave. Doesn't his master have him work and do the tasks assigned? Don't both master and slave expect the servant to put his master's needs before his own? (v. 8) And, when the servant has done what he

is commanded, does he deserve any special com-
mendation? Obviously not! *A servant's role is to
obey; obedience is nothing out of the ordinary for
him.*

And so Jesus applies the analogy. "You, too, when
you've done *all* that you are commanded, say, 'We
have only done our duty . . . we're not even good
servants'" (see v. 10).

What did Jesus mean? It should be clear. Jesus
had given His disciples a *command:* Rebuke him.
Forgive. This is no optional activity for men
with exceptional faith. This is the way every disciple is to live with others—obeying the Lord
whom he has determined to follow. Taking up
daily the cross of God's will. When it comes then to
living by Jesus' commandments, *the issue is not
faith—it's obedience!*

How this strikes at our excuses! We're so prone
to complain. "Oh, if only I were a better Christian.
If only I had extra faith. *Then* I'd rebuke. *Then*
I'd forgive. *Then* I'd reach out to love or pray for
my enemy." To such thinking Jesus has once and
for all cried, STOP! You need no extra faith to obey.
"Remember, I am LORD. It is for you to *do as I
command.*"

This incident revealed the disciples' confusion
about the function of faith in the life of a follower
of Jesus. It's a confusion that many believers share
today. While this incident does not give direct
teaching about what faith is, Jesus does settle one
thing. We can never draw back from doing God's
revealed will because we feel we have inadequate
faith. Or for any other reason. As servants of Jesus
Christ, we are to obey when He speaks.

But then Luke shows how Jesus moved on to
illustrate and teach the role of faith.

Faith's Functions
Luke 17:11—18:30

Obedience is one key to finding fulfillment in the disciple life. As we discover Jesus' will expressed in Scripture and impressed on us by the Holy Spirit, we can rejoice to know that we are free to obey. Enablement comes as we act.

But what role then is left for faith? In a sense, of course, faith undergirds obedience. It is because we know and have confidence in the One who speaks as our Lord that we choose to be His servants. But there is more than this to the disciple's life of faith.

Luke 17:11-19

Faith stimulates obedience. Jesus heard 10 lepers calling to Him from a hill some distance from the road. They stood away, as society decreed they should. Still they called out for mercy (v. 13), and in response Jesus told them to "go, show yourselves unto the priests" (v. 14). The implications were clear to the men. A leper who had been healed was told in Old Testament law to show himself to a priest, that he might be certified well, and to offer a prescribed offering to God (Lev. 13:2). *As they were going* (v. 14), they were cleansed. Because they trusted Jesus, they had not waited for the overt evidences of the disease to disappear. They went, confident He had met their need, and healing was theirs.

Faith is like this. It impels us to obey before we see the full evidence of God's working. Do you feel inadequate to rebuke, or to forgive? Then remember who it is that spoke to you. Remember Jesus' power and His love. Let that confidence encourage you to act, and *as you obey* His victory will come.

Only one of the 10, when he saw that his healing was a reality, paused. He turned back, praising God in loud shouts, and thanked Jesus. Only one found time to return. And he was a foreigner(v. 16).

Have you taken time to come back? To thank Jesus for your salvation, and your new life? Do you and I praise God that we have been healed within?

Our salvation doesn't rest on gratitude. Jesus said to the leper as He sent him on his way again, "Thy faith hath made thee whole" (v. 19). Our salvation doesn't depend on what we do *after* Jesus has spoken forgiveness to us. But how appropriate it is to come back joyfully to Him, with thanks and praise, to offer our whole selves, to be His willing disciples (Rom. 12:1, 2).

Luke 17:20-37

Faith provides certainty. We live in a world where things are not always as they seem—where, in fact, reality is often hidden by illusion. It is faith that frees us to see through appearances, and know things as they really are.

The Pharisees were men without faith. They insisted on testing reality by sight and senses. What they could see and feel and understand—only that —would they take as real. So they plagued Jesus. "When's this kingdom coming?" (see v. 20).

They were thinking, of course, of the promised Messianic glory, the outward show of power. The Lord knew them well. "The kingdom of God is not coming with signs to be observed," He said (v. 20, NASB). Instead, ". . . the kingdom of God is in your midst" (v. 21, NASB). How is it "In your midst" (or *among*, not *within*, as several versions translate)?

In the person of the King! Jesus, who stood before them, summed up in His Person all the power and the glory that one day will be displayed for all to see. But they could not see Him! The Pharisees saw only a carpenter from Galilee; only a dusty fanatic who had attacked them and their position; only a hated enemy whose miracles of healing roused their enmity instead of their compassion and wonder. *The King was there.* There were no outward signs of glory, but faith's eye recognized Him, and believed.

Sadly, Jesus turned to His disciples. He told of a coming time of trouble when they would long to see Christ's visible coming (v. 22), but that instead they would see Jesus suffer and be irrevocably rejected by their generation. There would be no outward signs of His return even later; life would go on afterward as it had in Noah's day (v. 26). People would be wrapped up in their own affairs: eating, drinking, marrying, going about the business of living in this world. Men would be unaware that just beyond the curtain of heaven, Jesus stands poised, waiting for the day when He is to be revealed to all as King, the day when He steps into history to judge!

If only people before the Flood had had faith to see in Noah's warning the reality, to envision the coming waters of destruction. If only the people of Sodom had had faith to heed Lot's warning before fire rained down. If only *we* understood that everything we take as "solid reality" today is destined for destruction when Jesus, the ultimate reality, appears!

It's this, the reality of God and His purposes, that faith's eye sees, and that unbelief is blind to.

How does faith help us, then? Seeing reality, the man or woman of faith acts. We flee the city of destruction (v. 31), leaving all behind.

As in every apocalyptic passage, there is in Luke 17:22-37 a concrete description of a real day to come. But of chief importance for us now is not to grasp each detail and fit it in the overall prophetic picture, but to see the impact of the whole. And to realize that it is faith, the confidence that God's word is *true*, that enables us to escape entrapment by the appearance of things now, to live in full commitment to God's values and by His standards of what gives life its meaning and its joy.

Luke 18:1-8

Faith motivates perseverance. Jesus often taught by contrast. He exposed the attitudes of others, and against that background His own love and compassion stand out. It could hardly have been otherwise. He was who He was; they were who they were. The vast chasm between the character of men and of God could hardly have remained hidden.

Now, He uses contrast in a parable on prayer. He told of a judge, cold and unconcerned about God's opinion and others' needs (v. 2). A widow appealed to him to right a wrong. He had the power and the responsibility, but he wouldn't act.

She kept coming. Everywhere he turned, she seemed to be there. Finally, in exasperation, he decided to settle her case. He still didn't *care*. It was only because she *bothered* him (v. 5).

Sometimes when we pray, we may get the idea

that God isn't listening. Perhaps we've prayed for a long time about something important to us. With no apparent response. How easy it is then to wonder: Has God heard? Doesn't He care? Why doesn't He act? Discouraged, we may simply stop praying, feeling that He doesn't hear or care. Or we may wonder frantically what we've done to prevent an answer; has sin cut us off from Him?

Jesus' illustration forces our attention in prayer away from *us* to *God*. What is He like? Is He an unjust judge? No! He's a Father, who loves us, and who does not delay but is acting speedily. When faith shows us the Person of God, we find quietness and confidence in prayer. We cry to Him. He hears. And He *is acting*. We may not see just now what He is doing and will do, but we can trust Him.

Faith, then, is a central thing in prayer. Faith moves us to persevere, not in desperation, but in the assurance that God hears.

Verse 8 asks a searching question. "When the Son of man cometh, shall He find faith on the earth?" May He find faith in us until His speedy return.

Luke 18:9-17

Faith frees us to kneel. Jesus' next parable speaks of the self-righteous, the man who prays with misplaced confidence. The Pharisee (vv. 11, 12) did pray. He came to God. But he only saw himself. His vision was clouded with the outward show, with the things he did or did not do. Self-satisfied and self-righteous, he saw neither God nor his own heart.

There was also a tax collector there, too ashamed

to even raise his eyes to heaven. Humbling himself before God, he found forgiveness (vv. 13, 14). And Jesus said, "It's always so. The one who humbles himself is lifted up; the one who exalts himself is brought low" (see v. 14).

The man who cannot believe that God loves and forgives will always turn to self-righteousness or to despair. Only faith, faith that lets us see God, frees us to discover and be our real selves.

Have you been hiding secret sin, even from yourself? Let faith's vision of God's love free you to fall on your knees.

Let the children come. What an appropriate climax (vv. 15-17)! Let the children come, that all may see the Saviour's welcome and realize that we must receive God's kingdom as a child. Why a child? Perhaps because we each must take our place before God, looking up, and realizing we see a Father's face of love. Perhaps, too, because a child, trustingly reaching out to take the Father's offered hand, is a timeless portrait of what it means to trust.

Faith's Object
Luke 18:18—19:10

Faith is a fine thing. But faith is not just something subjective, just something we "have." Faith is only as solid as its object, only as valid as what we rest our confidence in.

Luke 18:18-34

A wealthy ruler of Israel had listened to Jesus. Convinced that He was a good Man, the ruler posed a question: "How can I be sure of eternal life?" (see v. 18). Jesus probed to reveal the source of the blindness of this ruler, who saw Jesus as good, yet not as God, and who wanted to *do* in order to *inherit*.

Jesus stated the commandments that govern relationships between men (v. 20). The ruler had carefully observed them from his youth (v. 21). Then, with a single stroke, Jesus revealed the block that kept this man from faith. "Sell all that you possess . . . come, follow Me" (v. 22, NASB).

This was no condemnation of riches, nor was it a general command for all disciples. It was a skilled surgeon's deft stroke revealing a cancer. God spoke to him: "Sell all; follow Me." And the man went away.

He went away sad, for he was rich.

He chose his wealth over God.

And here we hear echoes of the first and great commandment of the Law: "You shall love the Lord your God with all your heart . . ." (Luke 10:27), NASB). Love of wealth had replaced love for God as the central value of this man's life. And Jesus' command revealed the fault.

As the man drifted sadly away, Jesus remarked to His disciples how hard it is for a man with riches to enter the kingdom (v. 24). Why? Because such men tend to misplace their hearts—and their confidence.

With God set aside in one's life, one seeks something else to have confidence in—his good works, his morality, his respectability, even his adherence to orthodoxy. Yet so many of our lives are empty today of Jesus' new life because we fail to admit that God is not *first* with us. That our ground of confidence has drifted, and shifted to become something other than Him.

The disciples were amazed (v. 26). They looked on wealth as a sign of God's blessing and approval. Who then could be saved? *Only those who look to God for what they cannot do.* Impossible with men, all things are possible to God (v. 27).

We must fix our faith in God.

He alone can do the impossible.

Luke 18:28-30

The disciples didn't understand. Still fascinated by the thought of the difficulties of the rich, Peter said excitedly, "We've left all to follow You! What will we get?" (see v. 28). Jesus answered them sympathetically. There would be far more in this world than they otherwise would have—and in the world to come, eternal life.

Luke 18:31-34

Jesus went on to speak of the great cost to Him of what we so freely receive. For God to do the impossible and give us new life, Jesus must die. But "the third day, He will rise again" (v. 33, NASB).

Luke 18:35—19:10

Faith's power. What can faith do? Faith rested in Jesus and anchored in God's love? The blind beggar whom Jesus passed by cried out and was given sight. How can we doubt that faith in this same Jesus can give us sight, to see and grasp reality (18:35–43)?

What can faith do? Faith placed in Jesus and anchored in God's love? Zacchaeus was a chief tax collector, one who rushed to see Jesus from curiosity. Jesus pointed to him. "Come." And as the Saviour sat at his home, Zacchaeus met the Lord. Zacchaeus showed the reality of the change in his life by repaying fourfold those he had defrauded, and giving half of all he possessed to the poor (19:1–8).

What a contrast!

The moral, rich ruler sadly turned away.

The scorned sinner volunteered to give away what had once been the center of his life. And Jesus said, "This day is salvation come to this house" (v. 9). Jesus had found another lost man, and he was saved.

What can faith do?

Faith in Jesus, a full-hearted confidence that frees from every chain and motivates obedience, can transform.

EXPLORE

To further explore this portion of Scripture and its meaning for you . . .

1. Jot down things you've felt you need greater faith to accomplish. Then reread pages 124-127.
   Reevaluate each item. What is the critical issue in each (faith or obedience)?

2. Look over the suggested functions of faith (pp. 128-133). Study each passage and jot down some way each principle can be (or is being) applied in your own life.

3. Reread Luke 18:18—19:10. Look at each individual described and try to identify the object of his faith.

4. Which of the individuals above do you feel you are most like? Why?

11

How Much?

Last year, I bought a new car, a Chevy station wagon. I mentioned earlier how hard it is for me to decide to buy certain things. The wagon seemed to cost so much.

That's one thing we need to face about discipleship, too. It does cost. Salvation is free, but to be a disciple is costly.

Zacchaeus (Luke 19:1–10) not only illustrates Jesus' power to bring newness of life, but he also introduces the theme of the cost of being a disciple. What did the disciple decision cost Zacchaeus? *Everything*. His life had been built on money. His goals, his purposes, his very identity as a person were built on the importance to him of wealth and material success. But suddenly Jesus came and gave him life. Zacchaeus responded, and *chose*. He gave away half of all he had to the poor, and repaid four times over any he had swindled. The core of his personality, the values that had given him direction in life, had suddenly shifted. Shockingly, *people* became more important than dollars. *Honesty* became more important than gain. Zacchaeus had become a different, a new man!

This is what discipleship will cost us.

What are your values? What is your life built around? What is your identity? Successful business man? Social leader? Popular personality? To the extent that what is important to you is not important to God, to just that extent discipleship will cost you. You'll give up what is important to *you* for what is important to *Him*.

This doesn't mean, by the way, that you'll necessarily stop being successful or pretty or popular. All it means is that these things will stop being so important to you. *You* will be different.

Discipleship costs. The next section of Luke raises the question of *how much*.

How much will it cost me to be a disciple?

And, how much will it cost me if I draw back?

Cost of Decision
Luke 19:1-40

Discipleship is costly to all of us, whether we choose its pathway or reject it.

Luke 19:1-10

For Zacchaeus, decision meant rejection of the old values on which his life had been based and commitment to the values of Jesus. Zacchaeus expressed those values in his behavior; he gave away the wealth he had once lived for.

Never make the mistake of thinking that you are a disciple simply because you agree with what the Bible says. Or go to church. A disciple is a person who has stepped beyond mere agreement to definite action. He has committed himself to *do*.

Actually, our actions always express our true values. Do we *say* that we have a heart for missions? Then how do we spend our money? Our actions express the values to which we are committed. We can lie even to ourselves about what we believe our values to be. But what is truly important to us will always show up in our behavior.

Being a disciple means we choose that which is important to Christ to be important to us too.

Luke 19:11-28

Immediately after the Zacchaeus incident, "as the crowd still listened attentively" (v. 11, PH), Jesus told another parable. There are three groups of people identified in the parable, and each illustrates something important about the cost of decision.

The working servants. One group singled out we might call the working servants. They identified themselves as the master's servants, and accepted the responsibilities to which he summoned them. Each was given a certain gift, with instructions to *use* that gift until the master returned.

What it cost this group was simply obedience: to obey the master's instructions. So each went out to work.

Again we see that discipleship is a costly thing. We aren't invited to warm a pew until He comes; we're charged with the *use* of our gifts and our talents.

When the master returns, the working servants discover that the cost was insignificant. The faithfulness of each is commended, and each is given opportunities beyond his dreams, and far beyond the value of anything he had gained for his master!

However great the cost of our discipleship may seem, the price is insignificant compared to the prize to be won!

The nonworking servant. This person also identified himself as a servant of the master. The *relationship* is not in doubt. But he failed to act as a servant should. He decided not to use the gift he'd been given, not to obey the master's command. Being a servant cost him nothing while the master was away, except perhaps the uneasiness of knowing he had disobeyed. But when the master returned, his choice not to obey cost him his reward.

It costs us much more to choose not to live as a disciple than any present cost might appear to be.

The enemies. There are some in the parable who have no relationship with the master. They have refused to be identified as his servants; they are enemies. And at what a cost to them! When he returns, their loss is the destruction of death.

What is the cost of a decision to be Jesus' disciple? Jesus' parable points up the real question: What will it cost us *not* to decide for discipleship? Only when Christ returns and reality is fully revealed will we know how tragic a price those of us who call Him Lord, and *do not the things He commands,* will have paid.

Luke 19:29-40

The next scene shows Jesus entering Jerusalem, riding on a young donkey, fulfilling the promise of prophecy (Zech. 9:9). And the Bible tells us the whole crowd of His disciples shouted joyful praises to God for what they had seen *Him* do.

Certainly this passage has great theological significance. Here, in Jesus Christ, God's promise of the Messiah's entrance into Jerusalem came true. But look for a moment at the disciples. See them shouting for joy. See them thrilled by all they had seen *Him* do.

And put forever out of your mind the dismal image of the disciple life as a drab and dreary existence or as endurance in hope of something better later on. Life as a disciple leads to joy and the thrill of praising God because a disciple, in living close to Jesus, sees *Him* do great things.

Cost?

No, discipleship is gain.

Analysis of Rejection
Luke 19:41—21:4

If the cost of discipleship is so light when measured against the prize and the present joy, why do people refuse? At root, rejection is the same whether it be the rejection of Jesus as Saviour by an enemy, or the rejection of Jesus as Lord by a believer. Looking further into Luke, we begin to better understand why some people hold back from God, or turn away.

Luke 19:41-47

Whatever the motive for rejection, such a decision is terrible tragedy. Jesus wept over Jerusalem and the destruction that would inevitably come upon the city (vv. 41–44). But tears are no sign of weakness. Jesus moved on inexorably into the Temple and expelled those who had defiled it (v. 45). Jesus cares . . . but the Judge of all the earth will do right.

Luke 19:47—20:9

The nature of rejection. In the Temple, day after day, Jesus confronted the chief priests, the scribes, and the other rulers of His nation (v. 47). These were men who claimed divine authority to govern and to rule. So they challenged Jesus' authority. "By what right do You act, where do You get *Your* authority?" they demanded (see 20:1, 2).

Jesus responded with a question. Did John the Baptist act with a divine commission, or was his activity purely human? And the men who claimed authority were afraid to answer. They feared the people, and finally confessed, "We don't know" (see v. 7).

What a picture. Men who pretended to speak with divine authority forced by fear to deny their own claims! With grand contempt, Jesus turned from them, and with firmness spoke: "Then I *will not* answer your question" (see v. 8).

What has happened here? *The authority of Jesus* (who has clearly demonstrated His power and openly claimed to be God's Son) *is being questioned.*

It is this very thing, the questioning of God's authority and the attempt to set up our own authorities (each of which is ultimately forced to make the chief-priests' disclaimer) that is at the root of rejection.

When we own Christ as Lord, when we willingly subject ourselves to His will, we have found the disciple's only antidote to the poison of rejection.

Luke 20:9-18

Rejection's motive. Why should people try to set up their own authorities rather than submit to God?

The parable of the tenant-farmers, who killed the heir to the vineyard saying, "Then it will be ours," gives us the answer. The motive for rejection is the desire to play God!

Lucifer became Satan when he rejected the authority of God and determined to raise his own throne above the throne of God (Isa. 14:13). Sin in us constantly throbs out the same message: I, not God, must control.

Yet how empty such usurped authority is. We may claim it by rejecting God's authority over us, but when we try to reach any of our life goals, we'll be forced to admit, just as the chief priests were, "I can't." How empty it is to insist on your own way, and then discover that apart from Jesus Christ's enablement you can do nothing!

And how dangerous it is to challenge God's authority with our own. Portraying Himself as the cornerstone, Jesus warned, "Every one who falls on that stone will be broken to pieces; but on whomever it falls, it will scatter him like dust" (v. 18, NASB).

Rush to challenge God if you will. You can only be broken or utterly crushed. Whatever your *claim* in your rebellion, the Lord is still God!

Luke 20:19-44

The futility of rejection. It's fully human to believe that somehow we are still able to make it on our own, that we really are strong, strong enough even to challenge God's authority.

Men from two of the groups that opposed Jesus came to challenge Him. Each relied on his group's strengths. And in each case, the strength proved a weakness.

(1) The chief priests and scribes (20:19-26) were men who prided themselves on their ability to adapt to changing political and social conditions. They had survived various foreign occupations; now they had survived under Roman occupation as well. Their watchword was compromise. When they came to Jesus, they noted His unwillingness to compromise on principle and felt that this "strength" of theirs would enable them to trap Him.

The people were totally antagonistic to Roman rule, and particularly to the heavy taxes they paid these Gentile oppressors. If Jesus spoke against taxes, they could report Him to the government and be sure of quick action. If He spoke for taxes, the people would turn away from Him. And because Jesus was not "strong" as they were, not able to compromise and fit in, He would be caught either way.

When they asked Jesus about taxes, He didn't even have a coin in His purse. He had to borrow one from the very men who were posing as anti-Roman friends of the people! He looked at it, asked whose features were stamped on the coins, and told them bluntly, "Then let Caesar have his own— but be sure you give God what belongs to Him!" (see v. 25).

Jesus had not compromised.

Instead, He had shown them that their supposed strength was really weakness. In their compromise they had surrendered what was rightfully God's—their total dedication—to Caesar in exchange for their place and monetary gain.

(2) The Sadducees tried next. These men were the "liberals" of that day. They believed this was their strength, this freedom from dead literalism.

So they confronted Jesus, a Person who had shown in His respect for God's Word that He was not as "enlightened" as they. They posed a question about resurrection . . . and they didn't even believe in resurrection! But Jesus answered them. He argued from the tense of a verb (God *is*, rather than *was*, the God of Abraham, Isaac, and Jacob) that these men were alive then, and not dead. He also explained that, in resurrection, marriage is no longer a part of our experience.

The scribes (experts in the Old Testament) volunteered, "Sir, that was a good answer" (see v. 39). Jesus had answered the "unanswerable" question, and maintained His full commitment to the Word of God.

And then Jesus posed *them* a question (vv. 41–44), a question that could only be answered by admitting that the Davidic King promised in Scripture must also be the Son of God! His challengers had no answer. They went away.

Have you realized that no matter what *your* strength is, if you rely on it, it too will prove to be your weakness? Are you intelligent? Do you rely on your intelligence to guide you through life, rather than seeking God's guidance and direction? This is rejection of God . . . and your strength when exalted above God will be your downfall.

Are you a naturally warm and loving person? Do you rely on your capacity to love, rather than asking God to shed His love through your life? Then be sure that your natural emotional responsiveness to people will betray you. You'll love unwisely, sentimentally, and make choices that will hurt both yourself and others.

You see, we are not really strong in anything. Only as we submit totally to God's authority, only as we surrender as disciples to His control, can we become the new persons we should be.

Rejection, then, is at heart a questioning of God's authority, motivated by a desire to have what is His—the right to control our life. And rejection, this claiming of control, is utterly futile. It is futile, for apart from Jesus Christ even our strengths become our weaknesses, and life proves over and over again that apart from Him we can do nothing.

Jesus Christ must have control over your life.

You must give Him control, or, in that area in which you demand the right to run your own life, you will not be a disciple.

And you will not be transformed.

Luke 20:45—21:4

What can we do? We can be like the scribes Jesus describes. We can walk around, pretending to be religious and dedicated, while all the time we're simply trying to win others' approval and letting selfishness control us (vv. 46, 47).

Or we can be like the widow, a woman who was set apart and honored above the wealthy who dropped lavish gifts into the offering for God. The widow was not praised because she gave little, but because she gave *all*.

This is what God wants from you and me.

Whatever we have.

Whatever we are.

Will we give all?

EXPLORE

To further explore this passage of Scripture and its meaning for you . . .

1. Make a list of all the things that you believe are truly important to you.
2. Now check each against your behavior. How do the things you do and decisions you make demonstrate these are important to you? Does your behavior indicate other things may be even more important?
3. What, from your study of Luke to date, do you believe is truly important to God? (Feel free to review as you make up your list.) Can you see any ways your behavior or values might change if these things were more at the center of your life?
4. Work through this section of Luke, and from the text develop a list of reasons why a person should or should not choose to be a totally dedicated disciple.

12

The Price
and
the Promise

"It's ours!"

Imagine yourself on an expedition into Arizona's
Superstition Mountains on the trail of the Lost
Dutchman. You enter a half-hidden cave, and
there on a ledge, covered by the dust of decades,
you discover a dozen old pouches whose cracked
leather reveals a flash of yellow within. You pick
up one of the pouches, and it breaks open in your
grasp, and suddenly a golden shower cascades over
you, tinting your hands and clothes with treasure.
Tense with excitement, you shout to your com-
panion, "It's ours! The gold is ours!!"

This is how Luke makes me feel. In it he has
shown us the true treasure—the priceless promise
of transformation that we can experience as we live
as disciples of Jesus Christ. Suddenly everything is
new and different; life opens outward to a thou-
sand glorious potentialities.

It's so easy for the one who *finds* a treasure to
forget the one who provided it. In that Arizona
cave, I'm likely never to think that decades before
someone had to work and sweat and dig to gather

the gold I now hold, that probably this same person died, or he wouldn't have left the treasure where I could find it.

Luke doesn't let us forget the cost of *our* treasure. Jesus Christ suffered, and died, to provide for me the promise of transformation. Luke 22 and 23 detail for us the terrible cost to Him of new life for you and me.

The Cost
Luke 22:1—23:56

We see several themes developed in these two chapters. We see the theme of suffering: of Jesus' agony expecting, and then experiencing, the cross —of Jesus' agony as the men He came to touch with love brutally beat back His outstretched hands. Again we see two themes in contrast: we see the theme of control (the Man dragged before the courts has the situation fully in His hands!) against the backdrop of human inadequacy (all those around Jesus prove weak, mere leaves swept by winds of circumstance). And we see the theme of finality: "It is finished." Jesus' work is done. Salvation is won!

Luke 22:1-6

The desperate hatred of the Jewish rulers in these last moments of Jesus' life takes form in a plan to kill Him, put into Judas' willing mind by Satan. The experience of being close to Jesus has not changed Judas' heart. He's held back—now he makes his decision to betray. Watch out when you hold back. "Close" doesn't count. The longer you put aside the decision for discipleship, the more likely you are to ultimately betray the Lord Jesus Christ.

Luke 22:7-18

While the plot is being made, Jesus prepares for the Last Supper, the Passover feast. The town is packed with visitors; yet no preparations have been made. So Jesus sends two disciples to find an empty room for them all. They watch for a man carrying a water jug (normally woman's work), and follow the man to find the room.

Jesus is about to die. But even the smallest details show that He is still in complete control of every circumstance.

At the dinner, He speaks of His suffering.

Luke 22:19-22

There, He also speaks of the purpose of His suffering: "My body . . . *given for you.*" "My blood . . . *shed for you*" (vv. 19, 20).

Jesus' pathway has been determined: He is committed to follow it to the very end. He follows "for you."

Luke 22:23-30

The disciples are insensitive. They don't understand what Jesus is saying, nor are they aware of His sorrow. They fall to arguing about who will be greatest in the days of glory to come.

Jesus remembers how these men have stood by Him through His years on earth. "Yes, you will sit on thrones and rule," He assures them (see vv. 28-30). But *now,* be servants.

Be like Me. Serve your brothers.

Luke 22:31

Now Jesus speaks to Simon. If Simon only knew how Satan has desired to have him. But Jesus has prayed. *The Lord is still in control.*

Peter is so sure of himself, so proud and confident in his commitment. "Why, Lord, I'll never leave you." Peter was sure nothing could touch his loyalty. He felt self-sufficient and able. But soon he would deny the Lord. Only Jesus was truly confident with a cause.

Luke 22:35-47

Jesus continued to warn His followers about the change to expect when He was gone (vv. 35, 36). Then He led the disciples out of Jerusalem to a garden where He prayed. He was in utter agony at the prospect of that next day. It wasn't the pain—but that the Son of God would, as He bore the curse of sin, be cut off from the Father. *But He never lost control.* "Your will be done."

And after prayer, Jesus moved steadfastly, ready to meet His destiny and doom.

Luke 22:47-53

Judas arrived with an armed mob and stepped forward to identify the Master with a kiss of greeting. Suddenly the disciples saw the danger; Peter drew a sword and slashed at the servant of the high priest, severing his ear.

Jesus stopped him. With a touch, He restored the ear, and then submitted Himself to these picked representatives of Satanic power. *He was not forced.* He chose to submit.

Jesus was in control.

Luke 22:54-66

Now the scene momentarily shifts to Peter, who in naive confidence had proclaimed his readiness to follow Jesus even to death. Peter *had* followed. While the others scattered, Peter trailed behind his Lord, and even gained entrance to the enemy's courtyard.

But Peter's bravery could only carry him so far. Accused of being one of Jesus' people, Peter denied it. Three times. And then as the cock crowed, Jesus, at that moment passing through the courtyard from room to room, turned a steady gaze into Peter's eyes.

With a sickening jolt, Peter realized what he had done. And he went outside and wept bitterly.

How sickening for us when we realize our inadequacy. How desperately we need to look always to Jesus—for Jesus is always in control.

Luke 22:66-71

Jesus now stood before the rulers of Israel after a night of brutal interrogation. "Tell us," they demanded, "are You the Christ."

"Ye say that I am" (v. 70), in the idiom of the day was not equivocation; it affirmed. Phillips makes the reply clear: "You are right. *I am!*" They understood. "We've heard it from His own lips!"

For them the case was closed.

Jesus must die.

Luke 23:1-12

Because the Jews under Roman occupation had no authority to execute, the leaders took Jesus to the Roman governor and to Herod, who ruled an area that included Galilee. Surely one of these might be persuaded to pass the death sentence.

Pilate, unhappy about the request because he recognized the Jewish motives and found nothing criminal in Jesus' behavior, sent the Lord over to Herod. How weak, this man with power of life and death. He lacked the courage to act on his own convictions. He was a prisoner of circumstance; the ruler was ruled. Only Jesus stands tall.

Luke 23:13-25

The return of Jesus to Pilate by Herod is even more revealing. The Roman ruler is actually ruled by his subjects! Against his own sense of justice, Pilate bows to the angry cry, "Crucify!" He orders the death of a Man he knows is innocent.

How clearly we see it here. You and I, whoever we are, are no strangers to weakness. We are no stronger than Peter or Pilate. Jesus *had* to die for us. He alone has strength enough and strength to spare. He alone is free.

Luke 23:26-31

On the way to the cross, staggering under the weight and pain, Jesus is both jeered at and wept for. He turns to the women who cry. "Don't weep for Me . . . weep for yourselves and your children" (see v. 28). The city of Jerusalem, which rejected and murdered her Lord, would soon be razed. Within decades, Titus and a Roman army would totally destroy the Holy City, plundering, and killing the citizens that disease and starvation left alive.

"Weep not for Me."

The burdened Saviour's strength seemed to fail. But He was in control.

Luke 23:32-43

They came to the hill.

The spikes were driven through hands and feet. The pole on which He hung swung skyward, and fell with a sickening, flesh-tearing jolt into its hole. Unable to breathe when His weight hung on His arms, the Saviour put His weight on the nail piercing His feet, and endured the searing pain to lift up His body to gasp a breath again.

Crucifixion.

Life, death, each breath, all a blaze of agony. A blaze of agony which *even now He chose.* He could have called angels to free Him.

But Jesus still was in control.

He chose to die.

Why?

The two thieves by His side knew why they died there. Yet, one ridiculed and mocked; the other believed. In faith this man cried out, "Remember me" (v. 42).

Jesus' answer came clear. "Today you shall be with Me in Paradise" (v. 43, NASB). In these two thieves, we see our whole world, for all men must find themselves identified with one of these two. Dying (for we are dying even now) do we ridicule, or do we say, "Jesus, remember me?" For those who take the step of faith, who see as did the dying thief the King in that third figure on the cross, there is the same answer:

"Today—Paradise."

New life!

Now.

Luke 23:44-49

All nature put on mourning, and as darkness flowed over the scene, the great work of redemption was complete. The veil in the Temple that had signified separation from God was torn from top to bottom. Jesus gave a great cry, and *He released His Spirit.*

He died.
Still in control.
His work done.

Luke 23:50-56

They took His lifeless body and laid it in a rich man's tomb. The body was wrapped in linen, the tomb door sealed. And on the Sabbath all rested. For the disciples, it was the end. Jesus, their hope, had died. Though they planned to minister to the body, packing it in funeral spices, their great dream of God invading history seemed forever gone.

And life stretched out ahead in empty years, years of struggling to live, of living by habit, long after the sense of purpose or meaning or goal had gone.

The Promise of Power
Luke 24

Jesus' death must have left His followers with a deep sense of despair and an aching awareness of the emptiness of life. If history's record had closed with the cross and tomb, life for us would be empty too, a brief experience of sorrows swallowed up by endless nothingness and night. But the tomb was not the end! The resurrection that followed blazes forth the power of God and demonstrates the amazing vitality that transforms death to life—the same vitality that can and will transform our death to new life, now.

Luke 24:1-11

At dawn on what we now call the Lord's Day, the women started toward the tomb with the burial spices. Their mood was broken when they found the stone that sealed the entrance removed, and two angels standing by the slab where the body had been laid.

Frightened, they fell, hiding their faces from these apparitions. But the angels spoke: "Why do you seek the living One among the dead?" (v. 5, NASB).

It was a good question. Jesus had told them often that He would die and rise again. *He had been as good as His word!* He was risen!

Have you realized yet that it is Jesus' resurrection power that God pours into you and me? That He makes us alive with Christ (Rom. 6:4)? That we do not have to know dead lives?

Let's not lie among the dead, going through the empty motions they do, trapped by the same frustrations, bound by the same inadequacies. Let's take Jesus at His Word today. He has come to give us abundant life. Let's trust Him . . . rise up . . . and *live!*

But when the women reported to the Eleven (vv. 9-11), the disciples were too disheartened to believe. Sometimes past tragedy or failure so colors our view that we can't even believe eyewitness reports of resurrection. Listen. Whatever your past experiences, *Jesus lives.* And because He lives, you too can live.

The resurrection of Jesus Christ is the proof of promised fulfillment. You *can* be transformed.

Luke 24:13-37

That day, the living Jesus met two discouraged disciples traveling home from Jerusalem to Emmaus. He chose to go unrecognized as they talked of the recent events and of death's end to all their hopes (vv. 19-21).

Walking along, Jesus began to show them all the Scriptures that foretold the necessity of His suffering and entry into glory (vv. 26, 27).

Today, Jesus offers us a present experience of new life. But everything we can experience is rooted in a reality and truth recorded in God's Word. *New life* is no mere existential experience for some. *New life* is a reality that is explained and confirmed in God's Word, yet that anyone can experience who trusts himself fully to Jesus Christ and steps out to be a disciple.

Luke 24:28-35

The two disciples on the Emmaus road must have been amazed and deeply touched as that third Man explained the Word. Eagerly they urged Him to enter their home (v. 29). As He sat at table with them, praying over the breaking of the bread, they recognized *Him!*

Everything changed at that moment.

It's the same for us today.

We may hear others tell of their new life.

We may read of new life in the Bible. We *have been* reading of it all through Luke's Gospel.

But new life begins when we see Jesus and

come to know Him. Our new life is found only in a personal relationship with Jesus Christ, the Son of God, who died for us, and who rose again. He lives *now* to make Himself real to you.

It's Jesus who *is* our new life.

And He *is* real.

Luke 24:36-53

The two disciples rushed to Jerusalem to share their joy. Even as they told the unbelieving disciples of their encounter with the risen Lord, He suddenly stood among them.

He showed them His hands and feet: death turned to life. He opened the Scriptures and helped them understand. And He promised them *power* (v. 49).

Luke's Gospel closes here, with this promise of power, and with the disciples' praise (v. 53). But for the disciples themselves, a new life had just begun.

All the New Testament, all history, bears solid testimony to the fact that these men and women were marked by a joy and power that turned their world upside down.

Luke can close the same way for you and me today. With power . . . Jesus' power . . . available now as we accept Him and choose to live as His disciples. And with praise—praise to God from each of us who comes to know in personal experience that Jesus' power truly does transform.

EXPLORE

To further explore this portion of Scripture and it's meaning to you . . .

1. What evidences can you see in the text that the Resurrection was a historical occurrence, not some "spiritual" thing?

2. Look at each group of people in this chapter who met the resurrected Christ. What changes did the realization of His resurrection make in their feelings? attitudes? outlooks? actions?

3. The chapter suggests several lines of evidence that Jesus' resurrection and new life for us is a reality. These are (a) the testimony of others, (b) the witness of Scripture, and (c) personal experience of Jesus Christ.

   How have these evidences been felt in your own life?

4. Experiencing the power of God for new life brings joy and praise.

   What have you to praise God for now? Why not take time to praise the Lord for what He has done, and for what He will do, in you?